GUIDE TO

Digital Photography

Shooting, Editing, and Printing Pictures

Explore

the world of

photography

with digital

technology

LearnDell.com

Lisa A. Bucki

ISBN: 1-59200-575-6

Library of Congress Catalog Card Number: 2004108259

Printed in the United States of America

04 05 06 07 08 BU 10 9 8 7 6 5

Thomson Course Technology PTR, a division of Thomson Course Technology
25 Thomson Place ■ Boston, MA 02210 ■ http://www.courseptr.com

To all of those in my family's photos.

Acknowledgments

Computer book publishing often moves so quickly that an author doesn't have time to enjoy a project. While this book also required rapid-fire delivery, its subject matter made for an unusually fun and challenging writing experience. It was really a treat to write about digital photography and working with digital photos, so I'd like to thank Publisher Stacy Hiquet and Acquisitions Editor Mark Garvey for inviting me to work with them on this project. Project Editor Cathleen Snyder did a terrific job in keeping the project flowing, as well as lending her editing expertise to catch and fix my brain blips. Copy Editor Gene Redding also provided vital language assistance. And Technical Editor Mike Sullivan did a great job keeping my feet to the fire. Thanks to all three of them for such great attention to this book, and thanks to Manager of Editorial Services Heather Talbot for assembling such a dynamite team. Full-color books like this one require extra attention, so I also would like to extend my appreciation to all the production team members, especially Interior Layout Tech Bill Hartman. Marvelous job, everyone!

About the Author

An author, a trainer, and a publishing consultant, **Lisa A. Bucki** has been involved in the computer book business for more than 12 years. She wrote *Mac OS X Version 10.3 Panther Fast & Easy, FileMaker Pro 6 for the Mac Fast & Easy, iPhoto 2 Fast & Easy, Adobe Photoshop 7 Fast & Easy, Adobe Photoshop 7 Digital Darkroom,* and *Managing with Microsoft Project 2002* for Premier Press, a division of Thomson Course Technology. She also has written or contributed to dozens of additional books and multimedia tutorials, as well as spearheading or developing more than 100 computer and trade titles during her association with Macmillan. Bucki currently also serves as a consultant and trainer in Western North Carolina.

Bucki started working in the photography medium when she bought a 35mm camera in the mid '80s for a college photojournalism course. She has used her skills to take photos for corporate newsletters and brochures. Since her family members learned that Bucki had acquired both a digital camera and a scanner, Bucki has tackled projects such as scanning and retouching family images from the early part of the 20th Century. Bucki's dogs Bo and Rika remain her favorite photo subjects, along with plants and wildlife.

All photos in this book were taken by Lisa A. Bucki unless otherwise noted.

Contents

3 Using Manual Camera Settings for Greater Control 35

4 Using Special Modes for Special Shots 51

Part II
Working with Your Images 61

5 Transferring Images to Your Computer 63

10 Sharing Photos Digitally 149

11 Transforming Photos into Keepsakes 167

Part IV
Exploring Further Possibilities 177

12 Taking Better Photos 179

Introduction

Afriend sent you a holiday card of a family photo. "Nice," you thought.

You clicked on a link to go to the photo gallery of family reunion pictures that your cousin set up. "Cool," you said. "Why can't I do this?"

You watched as another parent shot photos of the soccer game and instantly showed them off to other parents. "I've *got* to try that," you realized.

Once the curious realm of geeks, tech heads, and top photographers, digital cameras now sit squarely in the mainstream. In the past few years, digital cameras have fallen rapidly in price and have improved radically in imaging quality and ease of use. If you're suddenly thinking that digital cameras offer a practical alternative to film cameras, you're not alone. In fact, InfoTrends Research Group projects that worldwide unit sales of consumer digital cameras will reach nearly 53 million in 2004, with worldwide unit sales of consumer digital cameras expected to surpass unit sales of worldwide film cameras.

Let *Digital Photography: Shooting, Editing, and Printing Pictures* help guide you into a new world of digital picture taking and processing. With its clear explanations, easy techniques, and realistic full-color examples, this book delivers the key information you need to start taking digital photos and expand your digital photography skills.

Digital Photography: Shooting, Editing, and Printing Pictures gives you information and advice about buying a digital camera, as well as teaching you how to use automatic mode and other camera settings to take pictures. From there, you'll learn skills such as transferring your images to a computer, correcting basic photo flaws, using special effects to "punch up" an image, and managing your digital library. Finally, you'll learn to share your digital photos on paper or online, as well as how to develop your "eye" for better pictures.

If you want to capture more and better memories and learn how to make the most of them, a digital camera, your computer, and this book provide everything you need.

Who Should Read This Book?

Though geared for beginners, *Digital Photography* presents info that can be useful in a number of situations:

- If you're about to buy your first digital camera, this book will take you beyond the camera's user's guide. Your camera's user's guide typically will contain great detail about the features and operation of the camera, but it will not really give you much help in transferring your mindset from the film camera world to the digital world.

- If you've mastered using your digital camera's automatic mode and other basic features but want to go further into the "whys" and "hows" of using other features like controlling shutter speed, this book will give you guidance.

- If you're looking for "need to know" information about working with your images once you've transferred them to your computer, this book will deliver the facts.

- If you're looking for more ideas about sharing your pictures or composing better images, this book will jump-start your creativity.

Because this book is loaded with clear illustrations, you won't have to struggle to learn a process. The non-technical language also helps smooth the transition from newbie to comfortable user.

With each task clearly identified by a heading, you'll also find it easy to use the table of contents to find the steps you need. So, whether you want to work through the book from beginning to end or find just the tricks that you need, this book will accommodate your style and enhance your results.

Added Advice

Once you dig into a particular set of steps, you may prefer to skip any explanatory text that might slow you down. Where warranted, however, the book highlights key issues in these special boxes:

CAUTION

Cautions alert you to pitfalls and problems you should avoid.

NOTE

Notes offer more detailed information about a feature, food for thought, or guidance to help you avoid problems or pitfalls in your work.

TIP

Tips give shortcuts or hints so you learn more about the ins and outs of the hardware or software.

Definitions cue you in to key terms you need to know.

Finally, a Glossary at the end of the book lists definitions and other important terms for easy reference.

PART I

Getting Started with Your Digital Camera

1

Choosing a Digital Camera

In this chapter:

- ✦ Understanding how digital cameras capture images
- ✦ Looking at camera models, from basic to high-end
- ✦ Identifying key camera features
- ✦ Other features you might want
- ✦ Considering file format and image quality
- ✦ Adding necessary accessories to the mix

Digital cameras have been around for only a decade or so. As with other technologies, the first units were clunky, expensive, and not very robust in capabilities. Even though early amateur digital cameras cost $1,000 or more, they couldn't focus and they could only store relatively small images.

In contrast, today's digital camera shopper has dozens of models to choose from at prices ranging from $200 to thousands of dollars. Just standing at the camera display in a store can bring on a big dose of analysis paralysis. How are you supposed to know which camera will be best for you?

That question can't be settled until you've owned a particular digital camera for a while (and the answer might change over time), but this chapter will provide information to help you make a better purchase decision in choosing your digital camera. This chapter explains how digital cameras capture pictures, compares the differences between more- and less-expensive cameras, helps you identify the most important features for your needs, looks at additional features to consider, examines the question of file formats, and concludes with a discussion of camera accessories.

How Digital Cameras Work

If you've used any camera—even a single-use version—you know that you point the device at your photo subject and press a button to take a picture. When you use up all the film in the camera, you remove the film (if needed) and have it developed into negatives and printed as photos. Although digital cameras require you to follow a similar process and many digital cameras even look like film cameras, a digital camera works in a dramatically different fashion. Understanding how a digital camera works will better prepare you to choose and use your first digital camera.

Traditional film cameras work primarily via a mechanical and chemical process. Light enters the camera through the lens. When you press the shutter button, the shutter opens and allows light to strike the film, as shown in Figure 1.1. The image actually exposes upside down on the film, as shown in Figure 1.1, because the lens bends the incoming light, thus reversing the image. The light-sensitive film records the image on three layers for the three different colors that make up all shades of light—red, green, and blue. To develop the film, the film processor exposes it to chemicals that dye each of the color layers to create the full-color negative. From there, a separate process exposes light through the negative onto photo-sensitive paper, which is then also developed using chemicals to create a final photo print.

NOTE

An aperture in the camera also works along with the shutter to control the amount of light that hits the film. See the section called "Controlling Light Entering the Camera (Aperture)" in Chapter 3 to learn how it factors in.

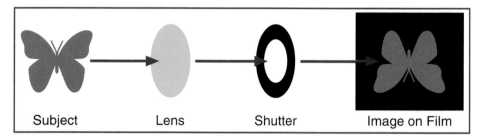

Subject   Lens   Shutter   Image on Film

FIGURE 1.1 A traditional film camera transmits light to film through the lens and shutter.

In place of the chemical part of the process for film cameras, digital cameras use—you guessed it—a digital process. With a digital camera, light again enters the camera through its lens and passes through a shutter after you press the shutter button. From there, the digital camera follows a different process to capture the image.

CAUTION

Another key difference between manual film cameras and digital cameras takes some getting used to. When you press the shutter button to take a picture with a digital camera, a delay occurs before the shutter actually functions. (This situation also existed with some highly-automated film camera models.) This means that you have to be still a bit longer when taking a photo with a digital camera, and you need to anticipate the moment you'd like to capture and press the shutter an instant earlier.

After passing through the shutter, the light falls on a sensor (called a CCD or CMOS) that reads the light photons and converts them to electrical charges. The camera then processes the electrical charges into a digital image, and stores the image on an internal storage medium such as a CompactFlash card. Figure 1.2 illustrates the image capture process for a digital camera.

The sensor makes a digital camera a camera. Each digital camera uses one of two sensor types—a CCD (*charge-coupled device*) or CMOS (*complementary metal oxide semiconductor*). Although there are nitty-gritty differences between the two, both work in a similar fashion. Light coming into the camera strikes the sensor, which on its surface

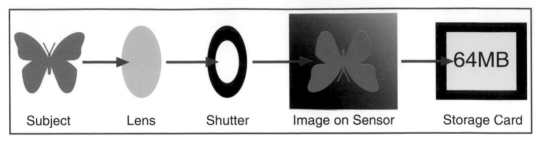

Subject   Lens   Shutter   Image on Sensor   Storage Card

FIGURE 1.2 A digital camera converts the analog light information to stored digital information.

includes diodes (called *photosites* or *pixels*) to read the light. The processing circuitry in the sensor then reads the intensity and color of the light striking the sensor and digitizes the light information into a pixel at the corresponding position in the digital image file, which can then be stored on the camera's storage card or medium.

> ***Pixel***, short for *picture element*, refers to the dots of colors that make up a digital image. The sensor in a digital camera also has pixels that pick up incoming light and convert the light to the pixels in the stored image. ***Resolution*** is the size of the image in pixels, such as 2,304×1,728.

The number of pixels that fit on a CCD or CMOS sensor determines the finished image quality. Over the past 10 years, manufacturers have been racing to fit more pixels on a smaller sensor chip. Previously, sensors used interpolation to calculate the colors that would appear in between the colors it could actually record. Some of today's sensors have so many pixels that they use little or no interpolation, resulting in a more accurate finished image. For example, the Fujifilm Super CCD SR chip is 1×1.7 inches in size, but it has a total of 6.7 million pixels, reducing the need for interpolation. The larger the number of pixels in an image file, the higher the printed resolution can be in terms of dots per inch (dpi). A sensor with more pixels enables you to save images that you can print at higher qualities and larger sizes. See the section called "Considering Image File Formats and Quality" later in this chapter for more about image resolution.

> ***Interpolation*** is a mathematical process for making an educated guess to fill in the gap between two values.

> ***DPI (dots per inch)*** identifies the resolution (usually the printed or scanned resolution) of an image in pixels per inch. *PPI* (pixels per inch) typically refers to the on-screen resolution of an image, as impacted by the number of pixels the monitor displays per inch.

Although at various times pundits have predicted that either CMOS or CCD sensors would dominate the digital camera market, today manufacturers continue to introduce improved functionality in both types of sensors. For example, even though they previously were used primarily on lower-end cameras, newer CMOS chips feature multiple layers that respond to light's wavelength as well as its intensity, increasing apparent resolution and eliminating the need for interpolation. One CCD model has both a primary and a secondary element at each pixel to better capture subtle changes in color and intensity. Yet another CCD not only reads red, green, and blue, but it also reads specifically for light green because human eyes pick up greens more readily.

TIP

The subtle differences in how sensors function not only affect image size and quality, they can impact overall image tint or tone. Some cameras regularly produce images with a red or yellow cast. It's worth the time to research whether a camera model that you're considering delivers lifelike color. Leading computer magazines and Web sites such as *PC Magazine* (http://www.pcmag.com) and *CNET* (http://reviews.cnet.com) review the newest digital cameras as they hit the market, as do photography magazines and sites such as http://www.photo.net, *Digital Photography Review* (http://www.dppreview.com), *Total Digital Photography* (http://www.totaldp.com), and BetterPhoto.com (http://www.betterphoto.com).

The image quality delivered by the camera sensor is typically expressed in *megapixels* (MP), with each megapixel being one million pixels. An older 2-megapixel camera could deliver images with nearly 2 million pixels, while today's more common 4- or 5-megapixel midrange cameras more than double the number of pixels. The megapixel rating, as determined by the capabilities of the camera's sensor, is one of the prime factors to consider when comparing digital cameras. As you'll see, the greater the megapixel rating, the higher the camera's price.

Comparing Pricey and Affordable Cameras

The range in megapixel ratings (sensor capabilities) serves as the primary determining factor of whether a digital camera costs a little, a lot, or something in between. As sensors improve, cameras in each range offer an improved megapixel rating relative to the price. As with other technologies, buyers have a tough choice—buy the bare minimum now and upgrade more frequently, or buy the best model that you can afford and use it for as long as you can. Beyond that, the price you pay will depend on how you plan to use the camera and what features that entails.

Least Expensive

Most digital camera models include a flash and can focus automatically. As such, most are considered "point-and-shoot," just like many film cameras, no matter what the price. Being point-and-shoot doesn't necessarily distinguish intro-level digital cameras from their pricier peers. Instead, digital cameras at the low end tend to have these points in common:

✦ A price between $200 and $400 or so.

✦ A rating between 2 and 4 megapixels.

✦ Light weight and a compact body, so the camera easily fits in a pocket or purse, as shown in Figure 1.3.

FIGURE 1.3 This Minolta DiMAGE X20 Ultracompact Digital Camera weighs only 4.1 ounces without batteries or storage card; Konica Minolta calls it the "world's smallest and lightest 2-megapixel camera."

♦ Possibly a fixed lens only, meaning that it has only digital zoom. With digital zoom, the camera mathematically interpolates data to increase the image size. This type of zooming often creates a blocky or posterized appearance resulting in a lower-quality image than with optical zoom.

With *optical zoom*, your camera's lens telescopes to change the focal length, which magnifies or zooms the image. The *focal length* determines the lens' magnification power. When a lens has a higher focal length rating, it can focus on objects farther away than a lens with a lower focal length.

♦ Possibly a smaller or dimmer LCD for previewing shots.

♦ Limited special features and modes, such as red-eye reduction.

♦ Ability to capture images in JPEG format only.

♦ A small storage card (8 MB to 16 MB) with fewer included accessories.

Midrange

Some midrange cameras might look a lot like their low-end cousins, but cameras in this category expand on basic point-and-shoot capabilities by offering more special modes and more manual settings. When you're looking at midrange cameras, you'll find:

♦ A price between $500 and $800 or so.

♦ A megapixel rating of about 5 to just over 6, yielding pictures nearly the same quality as a 35mm SLR film camera.

♦ A wide variation in body styles, from pocket-sized models such as the one in Figure 1.3 to larger models that resemble a 35mm SLR film camera, like the one in Figure 1.4.

♦ Heavier weight, typically more than 10 ounces without batteries and storage card.

♦ A better LCD.

♦ Better lenses that approximate a broader range of equivalent 35mm film camera lenses. Midrange digital camera lenses typically offer equivalencies between 35mm and 380mm. These cameras also offer special focus modes, such as a macro mode for extreme close-ups.

♦ Faster shutter speeds.

♦ Additional special flash and picture modes, such as snow and beach modes that correct for lighting.

FIGURE 1.4 The Canon PowerShot G5 offers 5 megapixels and both optical and digital zoom.

✦ Video capture and a burst mode. Many digital cameras can capture up to 30 seconds of video. Be sure to check which file format the camera uses for video—MPEG, AVI, or QuickTime—to ensure that you can use the resulting video files with your video editing application. Some midrange cameras can shoot 10 to 15 pictures in 10 seconds in burst mode.

> In **burst mode**, a digital camera takes several pictures in quick sequence after you press the shutter button only once. This helps the camera catch motion more effectively, giving a workaround for the delay between pressing the shutter and the actual shutter function.

✦ The ability to capture in multiple file formats, such as JPEG, TIFF, and RAW, as well as to choose multiple image sizes. For more, see the "Considering Image File Formats and Quality" section later in this chapter.

✦ Ships with a larger storage card, typically 32 MB.

Expensive and Professional Cameras

If you have years of experience working with 35mm SLR film cameras (meaning that you're not intimidated by terms such as *f-stop*) and you are chomping at the bit to use those skills on the digital side, the market now offers high-end digital cameras that aren't astronomical in cost. If you have an older point-and-shoot digital camera that no longer meets your needs, you might consider graduating to a top-level camera so that you have the right camera for any photo need.

1

When you whip out that credit card to buy a high-end or professional-level digital camera, here's what you can expect in return:

◆ A price of $1,000 to several thousand dollars.

◆ Megapixel ratings from 5 to 11 or more, with ratings of 8 becoming increasingly common.

◆ The look and feel of a 35mm SLR film camera, as illustrated in Figure 1.5.

FIGURE 1.5 This expensive professional camera, the Canon EOS-1Ds, offers 11-megapixel resolution.

◆ A larger, high-quality lens or the ability to change lenses, like with a 35mm SLR film camera. (You may even be able to use your lenses from your old 35mm SLR film camera, depending on whether the lens mounting systems are compatible.) A larger lens allows more light to strike the camera sensor, yielding better image data and quality. Digital cameras with removable lenses like a 35mm SLR camera often are called "digital SLR cameras" or "SLR digital cameras."

◆ The most control over manual settings, such as shutter speed.

◆ The trade-off of a much heavier and usually much louder camera. For example, like 35mm SLR film cameras, digital SLR cameras use the same lens for viewing (framing) and taking the picture. A mirror directs light to the viewfinder during picture focusing, and that mirror must be moved by motor or other means to shoot the picture. The mechanics to move that mirror cause noise and add weight to the camera.

◆ The best darn digital images you can create right now. An 8-MP camera shoots an image that can be enlarged up to 20×30 inches while retaining excellent quality.

SO WHICH CATEGORY FITS?

Your overall camera purchase decision—whether to buy a cheap digital camera, a pricey pro camera, or something in between—boils down to a key question. How do you want to use the camera? The answer can guide you to the right type of camera:

◆ Do you want to take basic snapshots at special events? In that case, you might prefer a quiet and light camera. If so, an inexpensive camera will do.

◆ Do you want to use the camera for a mix of shots, including some impromptu shots while you're on the go and some more artistic portraits of items and people? If so, look for a midrange camera, emphasizing the feature you want most (such as a high MP rating or better optics).

◆ Do you need to shoot low-res pictures for a Web site? You should be able to get it done with an inexpensive camera.

◆ On the other hand, are you shooting pictures for a four-color printed publication? If so, you will need a camera that can create images at higher dpi to accommodate the printing process. This type of camera falls in the midrange and pro categories.

◆ Will you be doing any professional work or serious volunteer work, such as shooting the official pictures for a soccer league or grabbing images for a church newsletter? If so, you need to plan to spend accordingly for a camera in the high midrange or pro range.

- Do you want high-quality prints of your images or enlarged prints (8×10 inches or larger)? If so, you need the extra pixel punch of a high-megapixel camera. Spring for a midrange or expensive camera with 3 MP or more.

- Will you be using your images for modest personal and home projects, such as photo greeting cards and small prints of 4×6 inches or smaller? In this case, you can probably get by with an inexpensive digital camera, especially if it's your first one.

- In contrast, have you delved into digital artwork using a program such as Photoshop, so that you need your own original digital content? If so, consider a better camera so you can get the image quality you want.

- Will the camera be used by you alone or by others in your household, including youngsters? If the latter is the case, an inexpensive, simple-to-operate camera will work best (and be less of a loss if it's misplaced or broken).

- Are you a serious hobbyist—in particular, a film camera hobbyist—who always goes for total immersion and mastery of a topic? Then buy the best camera you can afford. You won't be sorry.

Ask yourself exactly how you want to use your digital camera, and let the answer guide you to the right group of cameras.

Key Decision Features

Once you've narrowed your purchase decision down to a particular category of camera based on how you intend to use it and approximately how much you want to spend, it's time to start comparing similar models. Several camera features should rank high in priority when you're comparing cameras that you're considering for purchase.

- **Compatibility with your computer and its operating system.** Newer cameras might not be compatible with older operating systems, such as Windows® 95 or Mac OS 9.x. If you have any compatibility concerns about a particular camera model, check the manufacturer's Web site for information.

- **Optics and zoom capabilities.** The quality and power of the lens determines how much flexibility you'll have in capturing shots from varying distances. Compare the camera's lens focal length ratings, which will look like 38–114mm. Also compare the optical and digital zoom ratings, keeping in mind that optical (focal length) zoom is superior to digital (interpolated) zoom. Most midrange cameras have a 3× optical zoom rating. Pro cameras offer increased optical zoom capabilities up to 7× or 8×.

♦ **Battery type and life.** Be aware of whether the camera uses AA rechargeable batteries or a proprietary rechargeable battery, and compare the costs of additional and replacement batteries. Also compare the battery life of the cameras you're considering. If you plan to take photos at lengthy events and you want minimal downtime for battery changes, a long estimated battery life is important.

CAUTION

Some digital cameras, like certain Kodak EasyShare models, come with a rechargeable battery pack but also can use rechargeable AA batteries. In such a situation, you may be required to purchase a separate camera dock or charger to recharge the battery pack. Be sure to check carefully with the camera manufacturer's Web site to ensure you're aware of required add-ons for charging battery packs.

♦ **Storage.** Each digital camera model on the market today uses one of a number of storage media, with the Secure Digital, CompactFlash (see Figure 1.6), and Memory Stick media being most common. Some cameras, particularly at the pro level, can also use larger storage media, such as the IBM Microdrive. Some models even can save to 156-MB CD-R and CD-RW media. If you have other devices, such as PDAs, that use a particular type of media, such as CompactFlash, then choosing a camera that uses the same media type can help you economize.

FIGURE 1.6 Additional storage, such as this CompactFlash card, expands your camera's capabilities.

✦ **Interface.** Most digital camera models sold today can connect to a computer via USB. However, most use the older USB 1.1 standard. If your computer is equipped with the newer USB 2.0 standard, only a camera equipped to use that standard can operate at full USB 2.0 image transfer speeds (USB 1.1 cameras will transfer images more slowly). Some pro cameras even use the fastest available interface—FireWire.

✦ **Picture quality choices.** Some cameras enable you to make the most of storage by offering choices in the picture size and quality that you can take. For example, a camera might offer you the ability to shoot pictures at 1024×768 or 2048×1536.

✦ **Picture-taking and zoom modes.** Although the most basic cameras offer only an automatic mode for taking pictures, better models incorporate additional picture-taking modes, such as portrait mode, landscape mode, panorama mode, and night scene mode. Cameras also might offer additional zoom modes, such as a macro (close-up) or infinity mode. If you want to be able to take advantage of these modes, which enable you to set up the camera in a snap for any picture-taking situation, make sure you select a camera that has the modes you'll use most.

Other Features to Factor into Your Decision

If you still haven't selected a camera to buy based on the considerations already laid out in this chapter, then there are a few more factors that you can take into consideration to finalize your decision.

✦ **ISO equivalents and white balance correction.** If you're looking for a camera with great flexibility in accommodating different lighting conditions, review the ISO equivalencies and white balance correction settings it offers. A camera that offers more ISO equivalents will be more flexible. Some cameras also offer manual white balance correction and different white balance modes to correct for different lighting conditions—such as a tungsten mode for taking photos indoors or a daylight mode for taking photos outdoors—that can ensure you capture pictures with true color.

The *white balance* of an image refers to its apparent color temperature. For example, a photo taken indoors under fluorescent lighting often has a green cast, while a photo taken indoors under incandescent (tungsten) lighting often has a heavy yellow cast. If you have your camera's white set for indoor lighting and shoot outdoors, your pictures will likely have a blue tint. The top photo shown in Figure 1.7 has a bad white balance, giving it a heavy yellow tint.

ISO refers to the ISO (International Standards Organization) film speed ratings that have long been used to measure a photo film's sensitivity to light, with a higher rating indicating greater sensitivity. So, an ISO 100 film is less sensitive to light than an ISO 800 film.

FIGURE 1.7 The top photo would've benefited from white balance correction to remove the yellow tint of the warm indoor light. The bottom photo looks better with correction.

◆ **Ability to use filters.** Some digital cameras also enable you to attach lens filters that make color corrections or yield special effects. (The filters offer the added benefit of protecting the lens surface.) If you want to use filters with your digital camera, check for this capability.

◆ **Burst mode.** If you plan to capture a lot of action, such as when you are photographing sports, choose the camera with the best burst mode. As noted earlier in the chapter, the burst mode enables the camera to take several pictures in rapid succession, overcoming the delay that occurs after you press the shutter button.

◆ **Exposure bracketing.** If you're a skilled photographer, you've used exposure bracketing to ensure you get the right shot in difficult lighting conditions. Some digital cameras offer automated exposure bracketing for lighting settings, including white balance.

When you use *exposure bracketing*, you take a picture that you think has the right settings for lighting. You then take a picture that's underexposed (a bit dark) and one that's overexposed (a bit light) to ensure that you can choose the best image of the three.

◆ **Boot and recycle times.** The *boot time* refers to how long it takes the camera to power up when you turn it on, while the *recycle time* refers to the time the camera needs to reset itself between pictures. Although the boot time doesn't affect your use of the camera very much, the recycle time can. If a camera is slow to recycle, you won't be able to take as many pictures in a given timeframe. Recycle ratings might be a bit tougher to find, but some magazine reviews do include them. Also test this yourself by taking shots with demo camera models at a local retailer.

◆ **Docks and other accessories.** Some cameras include neat accessories, such as a dock for fast image transfer and charging the camera battery. If such a feature appeals to you (and you have the desk space to accommodate a dock that's always out), then you might want to choose a camera that includes a dock. Also, take the time to check into other accessories included with the camera, such as straps and AC adapters. You want to make sure the total package includes everything you need for basic camera use.

- ✦ **A self-timer.** If you want to take pictures that include your own smiling face, look for a camera that includes a self-timer. Some models might even offer two delay settings—for example, giving you two seconds or 10 seconds to get into the picture. Still other cameras include an infrared remote control, enabling you to take the picture at any time after joining the shot.

- ✦ **Output to TV.** If you want to show slideshows of your digital images on your TV for family and friends, make sure your camera includes a TV Out interface that's compatible with your TV.

Considering Image File Formats and Quality

Two last factors might influence your digital camera purchase decision—the file format the camera can use for image captures and the maximum image resolution it can create in dots per inch (dpi).

Inexpensive cameras can save images in only one format: JPEG. You have to be aware that the JPEG format is *lossy*. To save in this format, the camera uses interpolation to compress the file to a smaller size. In the process, some detail will be lost.

If you want the finest image quality possible, look for a camera that also can save images in the RAW or TIFF format (or both). These file formats are not lossy. Each pixel recorded within the camera is saved in the finished image file, resulting in better image quality. While TIFF images will include color corrections made by the camera, RAW images will not. Note that because these formats result in much larger files, they will consume more storage media space and may take longer to store to the media, increasing the recycle time between shots.

Also consider the image resolution that the camera can produce. A camera just over 3 megapixels can capture images up to a maximum of 2,048×1,536 pixels (3,145,728 pixels, or nearly 3.2 megapixels), which is enough for a photo-quality 5×7 print, or an 8×10 print with slightly lower quality. If you want to make larger prints, then opt for a camera with a higher megapixel rating. A 5.1-megapixel camera can capture images up to 2,592×1,944 pixels in size, enabling you to move up in print size.

TIP

Also, if you're using a camera with a higher megapixel rating and are in a situation where you can't zoom in enough on your subject, the higher image resolution will enable you to get better results when you crop the image later.

1

Must-Have Accessories

Finally, if you plan to give your digital camera heavy use right from the start, then it's worth including some accessories in your initial purchase.

✦ The 16 MB storage card included with most basic cameras can hold only about 40 1,024×768 images (with each image being about 350 KB in size). If you will be shooting pictures at a higher resolution or you want to be able to shoot for long periods without needing to change storage cards or move images to your computer, then buy one or more additional storage cards when you buy your camera. Storage cards range in size, including 32 MB, 64 MB, 128 MB, 256 MB, and even 512 MB. Prices vary depending on the type of media you purchase, but 128-MB CompactFlash or Secure Digital cards run between $40–60 before rebates. Prices have fallen drastically in the last few years, so storage will likely be even more affordable by the time you read this. Larger CompactFlash card (1G and above) also will be available, if pricey.

✦ A great camera bag is a must. You want to have extra batteries and storage at hand, and those items are inconvenient to carry in a purse or backpack. Further, the extra padding in a good camera bag will offer more protection for your camera hardware—which you want to protect, given your investment. Basic camera bags start in the $20 range.

✦ If your camera doesn't include a dock, one might be offered separately by your camera's manufacturer. A few manufacturers, such as Kodak, offer a dock that's compatible with a number of the manufacturer's camera models (which is why the dock retails separately). Expect to spend $80–100 or so for a dock. Kodak even offers a special printer dock that can print images directly from the camera for about $150.

◆ If you want to print images yourself, you'll need either a standalone photo printer or a high-quality inkjet printer. Quality printers start at $150, but spend more for a printer with higher print resolution to get the best prints.

◆ Keeping a digital camera clean can prolong its life and prevent damage, such as lens scratches. You can get camera cleaning supplies, such as lens papers, at your local photo supply shop. At least one manufacturer offers a digital camera cleaning kit with supplies for cleaning out the storage slot to reduce the chance of storage card read/write errors; you can purchase the Norazza Digital Cleaning Kit for about $20 through online retailers, such as Amazon.com.

◆ If you want to eliminate as much shake as possible, you might want to buy a tripod onto which you can mount the camera. Most midrange to upper-range digital cameras have a tripod mount (which is essentially a screw hole) on the bottom. Go to Dell.com to see the current selection of tripods.

◆ If you need more flash power to use with your digital camera, some manufacturers (such as Canon) offer external flash devices, as well as cables for controlling the flash and brackets for mounting them. These are pricey items that will probably appeal only to the serious hobbyist or pro.

◆ Most digital cameras (and computer operating systems) include very basic software for transferring and organizing your photos. However, the desire to play will soon take over, and you'll want to buy software to enable you to do more. For example, the Adobe Photoshop Elements software offers powerful image-editing capabilities, such as applying special effects filters to an image, for around $100. If you want to buy Elements as well as the Photoshop Album software for organizing photos, it'll run about $130. The Microsoft® Plus! Digital Media Edition package includes Microsoft Photo Story, a great program for developing onscreen slideshows of your images.

TIP

A number of camera manufacturers offer accessory, starter, or travel kits that bundle extra accessories you might want. For example, Kodak offers an accessory kit for its EasyShare cameras. The kit includes a carrying case, charger, an additional battery, and power plugs for about $35.

2

Taking a Basic Picture

In this chapter:

- ✦ Looking at the controls you'll use to shoot pictures
- ✦ Starting up your camera
- ✦ Using your camera's zoom
- ✦ Shooting a picture using auto mode
- ✦ Previewing pictures on your camera's display
- ✦ Turning the camera off when you're finished

Right off the bat, your new digital camera might look intimidating or even a little scary. For starters, it probably has a lot more buttons, settings, and doodads than the film camera you've been using—especially if you've been using a disposable camera! The various buttons and settings tip you off that operating a digital camera might require a trick or two that you don't know yet.

This chapter will help you break the ice with your new digital camera. Work through this chapter, along with your camera's user manual, to learn how to properly start, control, and zoom the camera; take a picture in auto mode and preview it; and finally, power down the camera.

Looking at Typical Camera Controls

Consumers have been transitioning to digital cameras in record numbers. To keep up with demand and to continue to push the technology envelope, manufacturers release dozens of new models every year. Recent models range from simple, sleek devices that are about the size of a deck of cards, to large, full-featured models that resemble professional 35mm SLR film cameras.

Depending on the model you select, your camera might have only a few basic controls, or it might have a smorgasbord of bells and whistles. The following list gives you a tour of the most common controls found on digital cameras. This list, along with the specific diagrams in your camera's user's guide, should help you become familiar with the controls offered on your camera model.

♦ **Lens and lens cap.** The lens gathers and focuses light and directs it toward the camera's CCD or CMOS device, creating the digital image. Some cameras have lenses that telescope out on startup, while others have a fixed lens. No matter which type of lens your camera has, always cover the lens with the lens cap when the camera is not in use. Unless your camera enables you to use removable lenses, there's no fixing or repairing a scratched lens.

2

◆ **Flash.** This lamp on the top or top-front of the camera provides light when you use the shutter button to take a photo. Chapter 3, "Using Manual Camera Settings for Greater Control," will explain how to use flash modes.

◆ **Shutter button.** You press this button to focus the camera and take a picture.

◆ **Mode/power/function switch.** For some cameras, this is a simple on/off switch to enable you to turn the camera on and off. For many other cameras, you move this switch to choose a picture-taking or playback mode, which automatically powers on the camera.

◆ **Exposure sensors and timer light.** These controls appear on the front of the camera. The exposure sensor checks the lighting in the photo subject area so the camera can adjust the exposure. The timer light blinks or pulses to help you count down when you're using your camera's timer feature.

◆ **Viewfinder.** As on a film camera, you can look through this window to compose your shot. Alternatively, you can use the LCD screen. The viewfinder might have crosshairs or a frame bracket to help you aim your shot toward the center of the desired subject area.

◆ **LCD screen.** This screen on the back of the camera serves a variety of functions. You can use it to compose a shot or to preview pictures you've already taken.

◆ **Rocker/controller button.** Use the four arrow points on this button to navigate through menus shown on the LCD. The control also might include an OK button at its center or an OK or Set button nearby.

◆ **Zoom.** This slider or rocker control makes the subject larger when you take the picture, enabling you to appear to be closer to the subject than you really are. Typically, working with this control actually changes the focal length of the lens, meaning that you're changing the optical zoom setting for the camera. To change the digital zoom, you use a camera menu setting.

✦ **Flash and timer controls.** Use these controls to choose the type of flash to use for a shot or to use the timer delay to take a picture.

✦ **Menu, preview, and display controls.** Press the menu button to display the camera's menu system in the LCD. Use the preview button to preview photos on the LCD. Finally, press the display (DISP) button to show settings, such as the date and time, on the LCD.

✦ **Operation and flash lights.** These lights typically blink while either the camera or the flash is powering up.

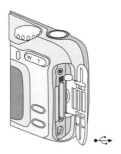

✦ **USB port.** Plug a USB cable (typically bundled with the camera) into this port to connect the camera to your computer.

✦ **A/V and digital out ports.** Use these ports to connect cables for displaying images and slideshows on your TV or a computer.

✦ **AC power terminal.** Plug an AC power adapter into this jack to run your camera on AC power rather than battery power. Make sure you only use the power adapter included with your camera or one that meets the camera's power specifications, as indicated in the camera's user's guide.

✦ **Storage card slot.** Insert storage cards (CompactFlash, Secure Digital, or Memory Stick) into this slot in your camera.

NOTE

The USB port, A/V and digital out ports, AC power terminal, and storage card slot can appear on either the left or right end of the camera. For example, many camera models have the storage card slot by itself on one side of the camera.

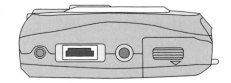

✦ **Tripod socket.** If you purchase a tripod to hold the camera steady for timer shots or more complex photos, the tripod screws into this receptacle.

✦ **Battery door.** Open this door to insert batteries into the camera.

✦ **Special connectors, such as dock connectors.** Special connections for devices such as a dock for the camera typically are located on the bottom of the camera because you sit the camera on top of a dock or cradle printer.

Powering Up the Camera

Your camera is like your TV, right? Just turn it on and go! Well, that's almost right. Unfortunately, because your camera doesn't plug in for power and it requires a few accessories to work, there's some preparation involved with starting the camera, especially if this is the first time.

Before you start your digital camera for the first time, you need to complete a few housekeeping chores to make sure the camera's ready to go.

✦ **Attach accessories, such as the wrist strap, neck strap, or lens cap strap, to the camera as instructed in the camera user's guide.** As with a film camera, these straps will help you work with the camera more easily under typical conditions (see Figure 2.1). For example, if you take photos primarily while sightseeing, using the neck or wrist strap makes it easier to keep track of the camera and to keep it close at hand for spontaneous shots.

✦ **Charge and insert the batteries.** Whether you're using a special rechargeable battery pack provided with your camera or rechargeables that you bought at the hardware store, plan on several hours or so to charge the batteries fully. Then, insert the

FIGURE 2.1 This camera has both a neck strap and a lens cap connector that must be attached.

battery or batteries into the camera's battery compartment (see Figure 2.2). Be sure to match up the positive and negative terminals of the batteries with the positions indicated by the **+** and **–** icons on the battery door. Close the battery door and slide the lock (if there is one) to the locked position.

CAUTION

Don't make the mistake of assuming that you should just use regular alkaline batteries. Being the power-hungry beasts that they are, digital cameras will chew through more batteries than you care to buy. It's far more cost effective over time to buy a battery charger and at least two sets of rechargeable batteries. For most digital cameras, that means buying a total of 8 AA NiMH (*Nickel Metal Hydride*) or lithium rechargeables.

✦ **Insert the digital memory (storage) card in the appropriate slot.**
Check the camera's user's guide to learn how to orient the card correctly and seat it firmly in the camera. Usually, this involves lining up a notch on the card with a notch on the slot or camera body, and then using gentle but firm pressure to slide the card in until the eject button pops up (see Figure 2.3).

FIGURE 2.2 Inserting a rechargeable battery pack.

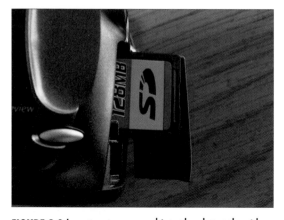

FIGURE 2.3 Insert a storage card into the slot at the side of the camera.

Once you've finished the one-time preliminaries, your camera will be ready to shoot. Follow these steps each time you use the camera to properly power it up:

❶ Take off the lens cap, if the camera uses one (other cameras have a retractable lens cover run by the camera). This step is a necessity for all cameras, because it prevents damage to the lens mechanism. If your camera's lens telescopes in and out, *always* remove the lens cap before you power up the camera; having the lens cap on while the lens mechanism is working can damage that mechanism. Some small camera models have what's effectively a lens cap integrated into the camera body. You have to slide the body open, typically by pulling the camera sides away from one another, which exposes the lens so that it can telescope.

❷ Turn on the camera's power. The method for doing so will vary depending on the camera model and manufacturer. For some cameras, you need to turn a power or function switch to the REC (record) or ON position (see the left image in Figure 2.4). For other cameras, you will need to move a mode dial to a position other than OFF (see the right image in Figure 2.4). Consult the camera's user manual if you need to find the specific method for powering on your camera.

FIGURE 2.4 To power on the left camera, move the mode/power/function switch to the REC (record) position. For the right camera, move the mode dial to a position other than OFF.

CAUTION

If your camera lens telescopes out when you power on the camera, be sure that the camera is not pointing down toward a table or other barrier. If the lens bumps a tabletop or other object while telescoping, the lens mechanism could be damaged or the lens could be scratched.

❸ Check the available power (battery capacity) and storage (pages or shots) indicators on the camera's LCD or in the smaller LCD on the top of the camera, if available. (You might need to press a Display or DISP button to turn on the indicators.) This quick check tells you whether you need to insert newly charged batteries or a storage card with more space before you try to shoot any pictures (see Figure 2.5). Your camera won't save a picture when the batteries are low or there is no storage space. It's usually less distracting to make sure the batteries and storage are in order before you get into the flow of picture taking.

TIP

Whenever you go out to shoot photos, put one set of charged batteries in the camera and carry the other set in your pocket or bag. Nothing's more disappointing than missing the shot of the day because your camera's out of juice.

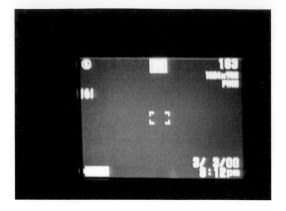

FIGURE 2.5 Always check the available battery and storage capacity, whether in an indicator display on the top of the camera or on the LCD on the back.

❹ Check other LCD indicators, such as those for image size, flash mode, and focus mode. Chapters 3 and 4 will show you how to work with specific camera settings like these. Getting into the habit of checking these settings will help you ensure you're always working with the settings you want for any given shot you take.

> **TIP**
>
> The first time you power on your camera, you might want to specify the time and date or the camera may require you to do so. This enables your camera to record exactly when you took each picture, information that may be valuable later when storing, organizing, and editing the images. Consult your camera's user's guide for the specifics of the process, which typically includes pressing a menu button to display menu options on the LCD, pressing arrows on a rocker button and a select button to navigate to the date and time settings, again using the rocker button and select button to set the date and time, and selecting the Set choice or pressing a Set button to finish.

Zooming In and Out

No matter what photo mode you use to take a picture with your digital camera, you need to zoom in and out to compose your picture—that is, to make the subject roughly the size that you want it to be in the final picture, as previewed in the LCD or viewfinder. Zooming with the zoom control sets the optical zoom, determined by the focal length of the lens. When you zoom a camera with a telescoping lens, you can see the lens moving in and out to reflect the zoom setting you choose.

To use the zoom control to set your camera's optical zoom after you've turned on the camera, follow these steps:

❶ Hold the camera up in front of you so you can look through the viewfinder or you can see the LCD display. If you use the viewfinder, you can hold the camera just as you would a film camera—in front of one of your eyes and very close to your face. To use the LCD, hold the camera with both hands about a foot or so away from your face so you can see the preview image on the LCD.

Make sure you pay attention to the crosshairs in the viewfinder or the auto focus frame (a set of square brackets that might appear in the center of the LCD) when you are zooming. You want to make sure that your photo subject is positioned properly relative to those indicators, whether centered or otherwise. Chapter 12, "Taking Better Photos," will give you hints on composing your photos and framing your subject for more interesting shots.

❷ Move the zoom control until the subject looks the size you want in the viewfinder or on the LCD (see Figure 2.6). A camera zoom control usually has a T at one end and a W at the other. The T stands for *tight* or *telephoto*, and when you move the zoom control thumb lever toward the T, the camera will zoom in on the subject. The W stands for *wide* or *wide-angle*, and when you move the zoom control thumb lever toward the W, the camera will zoom out on the subject, making it appear smaller.

FIGURE 2.6 Move the thumb lever or press the rocker button zoom control to change the zoom setting.

Once you're comfortable working with the zoom control, you're ready to move on and shoot your first pictures.

Using Automatic Mode to Take a Picture

When manufacturers made the first film cameras that featured automatic exposure and automatic focus, consumers went nuts for them. You no longer had to have the skills of Ansel Adams to understand how to use a quality camera. Finally, the average user could point, shoot, and get a great picture.

Being relatively smart cookies, digital camera manufacturers have made sure to include an auto mode (or automatic mode) on their digital camera models. Even better, automatic mode usually is the default setting for most cameras. Automatic mode sets the focus, flash (on some cameras), and exposure for you. All you have to do from there is hold the camera steady and take the picture.

> **NOTE**
>
> Some cameras use another name for automatic mode, such as "normal mode." Or, your camera may offer P mode (program mode) or AE (automatic exposure) mode, which chooses the best exposure settings, but still enables control of other settings like white balance. Some cameras have both an automatic mode and a program mode. Consult your camera's user's guide if you're not sure which mode is the automatic mode for your camera.

Follow these steps to use automatic mode to take a picture:

1. Power up the camera as described in the "Powering Up the Camera" section.
2. Use the zoom control as described in the "Zooming In and Out" section to compose the picture, using the LCD screen to preview the picture. (The viewfinder typically doesn't show you image focus.)
3. Press the shutter button about halfway down until the camera beeps and you see the image come into focus on the LCD. (In Figure 2.7, the shutter button is actually the silver button above and to the right of the mode dial. For other cameras, the shutter button may be in the center of the mode/power/function switch.) On some cameras, the auto focus frame will also change colors after the camera auto focuses. For example, the frame might turn green if the camera focused successfully or red if it did not.

FIGURE 2.7 Press the shutter button halfway to use automatic mode to set the exposure and focus.

If the camera gives an indication that it did not focus successfully or if you don't like how the image focus looks on the LCD, try changing the zoom slightly and then repeating Step 3. Or, if the LCD goes black, it may have gone to sleep due to power saver settings on the camera. Press the OK button or another button to "wake up" the LCD. Consult your camera's user's guide to see how to change power settings.

④ Press and hold the shutter button for about a second, until the image freezes in the viewfinder and you hear a double or triple beep. (In some cases, you can change the sound used to indicate the shutter action; consult the camera's user's guide to learn more.) This signals that the camera has stored the image so you can move on and take another shot. If the LCD goes black for a few seconds or more, that means the camera is still writing the image to the storage media. This can occur when taking very high resolution shots. When the image preview reappears on the LCD, you can take your next picture.

NOTE

Depending on your camera's capabilities and the image size you've selected (more on that in Chapter 3), there may be a lag while the camera stores the image content to the storage medium. To verify that the camera has actually stored an image, watch the LCD preview. After the storage process finishes, the stored image will appear on the LCD.

WHEN AUTO FOCUS MIGHT NOT WORK AND WHAT TO DO ABOUT IT

Some cameras use an infrared beam to detect a subject's distance from the camera when setting the focus. On other cameras, the auto focus feature seeks out the brightest area in the center of the scene and uses that brightness to set the focus relative to contrasting areas (because the subject is typically lit from the front). As a result, auto focus might not work correctly (for example, focusing on the wrong object) when you're trying to shoot these kinds of subjects:

✦ **Subjects and objects that are *backlit*, where the brightest light source is behind them.** Try to eliminate the backlighting (by closing a blind or curtain or turning off a lamp, for example) or use a manual flash setting, as described in Chapter 3. Or, move in close to the subject, use the focus lock feature described in the section called "Controlling Focus" in Chapter 3 to lock in a focus reading, and then step back and take the picture.

✦ **Objects with a strong glare or reflection, such as windows or metal surfaces.** Try to change the angle of the camera relative to the subject or object. Or, try to eliminate or moderate the light source that's causing the glare by adjusting the lighting or perhaps having a friend hold up a large sheet or other item to cast a shadow on the glare.

- **Surfaces with little shape or contrast, such as an interior wall.** If the surface has some texture, try placing a light source at an extreme angle relative to the surface to create more pronounced shadowing.

- **Repeating objects that are each brightly lit or brightly lit objects placed at varying distances from the camera.** Simplify the composition by focusing on one of the objects.

- **Poorly-lit objects, where the camera can't really find any light source.** Add a light source and some flash.

In addition, you might find that auto focus doesn't work properly if the camera is shaking, especially in low light conditions. In such cases, consider using a tripod, which you can buy at a local camera shop or perhaps pick up for a bargain at a pawn shop. Or, focus the camera manually, as described in Chapter 3.

Using Playback Mode to View a Picture

Once you've taken some digital pictures, you might want to pause to preview them. You can do so using the LCD display on the back of the camera.

TIP

It's a good idea to preview your pictures before you move away from your current subject or location. The preview will help you decide whether you've taken the right shot or perhaps you should try another angle.

Follow these steps to preview the images stored in your camera's memory.

1. If you're previewing pictures in your home or office after the actual photo-shooting session, plug the camera into a power source using the AC adapter that came with the camera. This step saves battery power and lets you preview pictures even when the battery is dead.

2. Move the mode/power/function switch to the PLAY (playback) position or turn the camera on in any mode and then press your camera's button for previewing images (such as the Review button on some Kodak models). If your camera has a telescoping lens, it will typically retract at this point, so you can put on the lens cap.

3. While viewing the LCD on the back of the camera, press the desired arrow on the rocker/controller button to move forward or backward between shots (see Figure 2.8).

4. When you've finished previewing shots, use the mode/power/function switch to resume taking pictures or to power the camera down, as described in the next section.

FIGURE 2.8 After you've entered the mode for playing or reviewing pictures you've taken, use the rocker/controller button to advance through the shots.

TIP

Some cameras enable you to delete images during playback or review. For example, when I display an image on my camera, I can press the Preview button and then select Yes to delete it. Consult your camera's user's guide to see whether your camera offers this feature.

Powering Down the Camera

You can't remind yourself often enough that digital cameras consume a lot of battery power. That means whenever you're not shooting or previewing pictures, you should take a moment to power down the camera.

FIGURE 2.9 The OFF setting powers down the camera.

1. Move the mode/power/function switch to the OFF position (see Figure 2.9). If your camera has a telescoping lens, it will retract and the camera will power down.

2. Put the lens cap on! Always do this just after powering down to protect the integrity of the lens.

TIP

Many mid- to high-end cameras offer power conservation settings. For example, the camera might have a setting that tells it to power off (or turn off the LCD) after a time length that you specify to conserve battery power. Consult your camera's user's guide to see how to use its power conservation features.

Using Manual Camera Settings for Greater Control

In this chapter:

- ✦ Choosing an image size and resolution
- ✦ Using flash settings to work in different lighting conditions
- ✦ Changing to the manual focus mode for focus control
- ✦ Using aperture priority mode
- ✦ Using shutter priority mode
- ✦ Quickly compensating for exposure
- ✦ Using the digital zoom feature of your camera

In the last chapter, you saw how to take a simple point-and-shoot picture using a digital camera's automatic mode. On some older digital cameras or the simplest and cheapest models available now, that's *all* you can do. However, the vast majority of digital cameras don't stop you there.

You can choose a variety of settings and modes to give you more precise control over how the camera captures images in a variety of conditions. For example, if you're taking photos outdoors and you never want to use the flash, you can turn it off. Or, if the automatic focus feature isn't focusing the image as you want, you can turn it off and focus your camera manually. This chapter shows you how to evaluate when automatic mode may not produce the best picture, and how to use your camera's manual features to compensate for the situation.

Controlling Size and Resolution

As you learned in Chapter 1, each digital camera can capture images at a maximum resolution, measured in ppi (*pixels per inch*). However, many digital cameras also enable you to choose images with a smaller resolution and/or lower quality settings to yield a smaller image file size.

For example, a camera might offer two resolutions (such as 2,048×1,536 and 1,024×768), as well as three quality settings (such as Fine, Normal, and Economy). For such a camera, choosing the 2,048×1,536 resolution setting and the Normal quality setting would yield a 1-MB image; changing to the 1,024×768 resolution and the Economy quality setting would yield images only 150 KB in size.

Other cameras offer only a quality setting, enabling you to specify the megapixel rating you want to use to shoot images. For example, the Kodak EasyShare DX4530 gives you the option of shooting images at Best quality (5.0 MP), Best 3:2 quality (4.5 MP), Better quality (3.0 MP), or Good quality (1.2 MP).

You need to think about two considerations when choosing image resolution and/or quality. The first and less significant consideration is the amount of storage you have in your camera. If your storage card is small, lower image resolution and quality settings will enable you to save more images before you have to change cards or move the images to your computer.

Second and much more importantly, think about how you want to use your images. If you only want to publish the images on a Web page, share them in an online album, e-mail them, or make small prints (4×6, for example), then you can choose a smaller resolution or a lower quality setting. On the other hand, if you want top-quality prints of your photos at the largest size possible, choose the best resolution and/or quality setting and just stock up on more memory cards. The Best quality setting for the EasyShare DX4530 mentioned earlier saves images that can be printed at sizes up to 20×30.

The process for changing the resolution and/or quality setting will vary slightly depending on your camera model, so consult your camera's user manual for the specifics. The following steps give you a general overview of the process:

1. Power up the camera.
2. Press the Menu button, typically found on the back of the camera.
3. Press the down arrow on the rocker/controller button (also on the back of the camera) to scroll down to the size/quality or picture quality setting category.
4. Press the OK button (often found in the center of the rocker/controller button) or the right arrow on the rocker/controller button. The available settings will be listed, like the ones shown in Figure 3.1.
5. Press the down arrow button on the rocker/controller button to scroll down to the desired setting.
6. Press the OK button or the Set button.
7. If a submenu appears, use the down arrow and OK/Set to make the final selection.
8. Adjust other picture settings, and compose and take pictures.

FIGURE 3.1 Choose a picture quality mode based on how you plan to use your image. Choose the highest resolution and quality to enable you to print images at a large size.

Controlling Flash

Because cameras capture and interpret light, the lighting hitting any subject can make a huge impact in the quality of a digital camera image.

For example, Figure 3.2 shows a shot of a cake shaped like a fish, taken indoors in the evening. Because no flash was used, the colors and background look flat and lack contrast. (That is, the image was underexposed.) Using a flash would've improved the picture.

FIGURE 3.2 This indoor shot needed flash to pump up the colors of the cake.

Exposure refers to the amount and intensity of light allowed to pass through the camera lens to the film or sensor, based on various camera settings, to create an image. When an image has been *underexposed*, too little light passed through, and the image will tend to be flat and dull with loss of detail because the photo is too dark overall. *Overexposure* is the opposite—too much light passed through, causing either unwanted heavy shadows or, more typically in digital photography, washing out the image with white light.

On the other hand, consider the shot of a bonfire in Figure 3.3, taken outdoors at night. Because the subject itself emitted plenty of light, the flash was unnecessary.

Most digital cameras offer at least four flash modes to enable you to compensate for various lighting conditions when you are taking your photos. Camera manufacturers even use standard icons to identify the currently selected mode. The icon for the mode you select will appear on the LCD on the back of the camera, as well as on the indicator

FIGURE 3.3 The subject itself, a bonfire, supplies the light source for this outdoor shot.

display (if any) on the top of your camera. Here are the typical flash modes found on entry-level to midrange digital cameras, and what the modes are used for.

- **Auto Flash.** The camera senses the lighting and fires the flash only when required.

- **Off.** Turns the flash off for all shots. Use this setting when you're confident that the lighting conditions will yield the type of exposure you want.

- **Fill or Flash On.** Tells the camera to use the flash for all shots. You might even need to use this setting outdoors on a sunny day. To learn why, see the sidebar called "What Are Backlighting and Fill Flash?"

- **Red-Eye.** In most cases, this mode causes the flash to fire twice. The first flash helps the subject's eyes get used to the light, so they'll look more natural during the second flash, when the camera actually shoots the picture. Some cameras continue to monitor light conditions in red-eye mode and will flash only once or not at all depending on the surrounding light. Also keep in mind that this mode works best when the subject is looking directly at the camera.

When a photo has been marred by *red-eye*, the human or animal subject's eyes have an unnatural red or green glow. This happens because the flash lighting bounces off the back of the eyes.

When you want to choose a flash setting to use for your next shots, follow these steps:

1. Power up the camera.
2. Press the flash control button, which has an icon like a lightning bolt and is typically found on the top of the camera, as many times as necessary to display the icon for the desired flash mode in the LCD preview and/or indicator display.
3. Press the OK or Set button if required by your camera.
4. Pause until the flash ready indicator light (a green light beside the flash unit) comes on or stops flashing.
5. Adjust other picture settings as desired, and compose and take pictures.

There's one more thing to think about when you're using your flash. Every flash has an effective range, based on the power of the flash's lamp. For entry-level to midrange cameras, the effective flash range typically runs from 2 to 12 feet or so. The effective range also can be affected by other camera settings, such as whether you're working in telephoto/tight focus or wide angle/wide focus. So, consult your camera's user manual to ensure you know how close you must be to your subject for the flash to be effective.

WHAT ARE BACKLIGHTING AND FILL FLASH?

Certain lighting conditions routinely challenge even more experienced photographers and factor into whether you should use one of your digital camera's flash modes for a shot.

Under very bright light conditions outdoors, an image can be overexposed, making the detail areas too dark. This can also happen indoors, where focused lighting on a subject in an otherwise dark room can cause high contrast and deep shadows. Using some flash (called using *fill flash*) can "fill in" the dark areas, making the detail more apparent. Figure 3.4 illustrates a subject taken indoors, with and without fill flash.

Fill flash also can help when *backlighting* mars an image—in other words, too much light behind the subject causes it to appear overly dark and with loss of detail against a too-bright background.

Using fill flash can be a little tricky. The right image in Figure 3.5 actually has a bit too much flash, because even midrange digital cameras only provide one or two settings for using flash. Higher-end cameras provide additional flexibility in setting flash intensity, so a photographer can apply the correct amount of flash in various situations. To overcome the limitations of your camera's flash, you can work with other exposure settings, such as using aperture priority mode to specify the amount of light entering the camera, as described in the "Controlling Light Entering the Camera (Aperture)" section later in this chapter.

3

FIGURE 3.4 In the left picture, you can't see the details of the figurine because of the heavy shadows. Flash helped bring those details out (fill them in) in the right image.

FIGURE 3.5 In the left picture, the orchid looks dark due to the backlighting coming through the window behind it. You can see the flower's details in the right image, which was shot with flash.

Controlling Focus

Most digital camera users really benefit from the auto focus capabilities of today's digital cameras. The auto focus feature enables the camera to focus automatically on the item in the focus frame (in the viewfinder or LCD) or foreground when you press the shutter button halfway down. However, because the auto focus feature in part depends on surrounding lighting conditions and tends to focus the camera on the brightest object in the scene, it can sometimes prevent you from taking the image you want.

Figure 3.6 shows an example of what can happen when you use auto focus. The auto focus locked in on the lighter background, rather than the real subject of the image—the dark foliage in the foreground. In a situation like this, you might want to use your camera's manual focus mode, if available, to take control of focusing the camera yourself. (Or, try the focus lock feature detailed in a later tip.)

FIGURE 3.6 Auto focus created a problem in this image because it focused on the lighter background rather than the dark foliage in the foreground.

Follow these steps to use the manual focus for your camera:

1. Power up the camera.
2. Choose a picture-taking mode and other settings.
3. Press the focus control button, often found on the top of the camera, as many times as necessary to display the icon for the manual focus mode in the LCD preview and/or indicator display. This icon typically looks like **MF**.
4. Compose the picture.
5. Looking through the viewfinder or at the LCD preview, use the camera's focus controls to focus the picture as desired. The focus controls vary quite a bit. For example, on some cameras, you press the left and right arrow

buttons on the rocker/controller button. One of the newest high-end digital camera models from Sony offers the same type of focus control as traditional 35mm SLR cameras—twisting the lens barrel to achieve the desired focus.

CAUTION

Some digital cameras give you only a limited period of time to use the manual focus. For example, you might have to focus the camera while the **MF** indicator is flashing.

⑥ Press the shutter to record the picture.

NOTE

Your digital camera might offer another tool for overriding auto focus mode—a focus lock feature. Focus lock enables you to focus the camera on an object, lock the current focus setting, and then direct the camera at another subject to take its picture instead. Typically, locking the focus also locks the exposure settings. It's usually simple to use focus lock. Choose other picture settings as needed, and point the camera at the subject so the subject appears in the auto focus frame on the LCD. Press and hold the shutter button halfway down until the auto focus frame indicates (usually by changing colors) that the camera has focused. Continue holding the shutter button halfway down, point to the new subject, and then press the shutter button all the way to record the shot.

Controlling Light Entering the Camera (Aperture)

You've already learned that the amount of light entering a camera results in the exposure of the finished image. Two camera settings control the exposure—the aperture size setting and shutter speed setting. Your camera's automatic mode changes the aperture size and shutter speed automatically to set the exposure for a picture. However, many digital cameras give you the option of setting either the aperture size or shutter speed manually, to achieve other effects in a picture. This section focuses on the aperture priority mode, in which you choose the aperture size to use for a picture, while the camera selects the shutter speed automatically. (Skip to the next section to learn more about using shutter priority mode.)

The aperture, found along with the shutter between the lens and the sensor in a digital camera, is made of a number of pieces of thin material positioned in a circular formation so that they form a circular opening in the center. The aperture's parts move to change the size of the circular opening to admit more or less light as needed, much like the iris of an eye, while the shutter is open. (That's why an aperture is sometimes called an *iris diaphragm*.) The aperture size thus contributes to a particular exposure by allowing more or less light through to hit the camera sensor.

Digital camera manufacturers have continued the traditional method of expressing aperture size as f-stop values. f-stop settings are expressed like this: f/2, f/2.8, f/4, f/5.6, f/8, f/11, and so on. The lower f-stop values indicate a larger aperture size (a larger opening), allowing more light in to expose the image.

NOTE

If your digital camera has a full manual mode, you can choose it to set both f-stop and shutter speed to have full control over the exposure. In such a case, you might choose a lower f-stop value when shooting indoors or outdoors on an overcast day to get a fully exposed picture without having to use the flash. (Flash lighting can sometimes look harsh.) On the other hand, choose a higher f-stop value when you are shooting outdoors in bright sunlight to avoid overexposing the image.

CAUTION

Even though your digital camera adjusts the shutter speed to offset the f-stop you select and create a correct exposure, using aperture priority mode can affect the overall exposure. Photos taken at lower f-stop settings can be overexposed in sunny outdoor conditions.

In addition to affecting the amount of light entering the camera, the f-stop setting you choose in aperture priority mode has another effect you should consider. Lower f-stop settings narrow the range of focus (also called the *depth of field*) for the picture. For example, if you choose a higher f-stop, your camera might be able to focus well on subjects 2 to 50 feet away from the camera, but with a lower f-stop it might only focus well in the two- to five-foot range. (The focal length of the lens also affects depth of field.) Figure 3.7 illustrates this effect. Both images were shot in the close-up or macro focus mode, with aperture priority mode as the picture mode. The top image was shot at f/4, and the bottom image was shot at f/8. Notice how the leaves and blooms in the lower-left corner of the top image are somewhat fuzzy, but they appear crisper in the bottom image. That's because the lower f-stop setting used for the top image narrowed the focus range.

FIGURE 3.7 These pictures were shot in aperture priority mode at f/4 and f/8, respectively. Observe the lower-left area of the image to see the difference in focus in the leaves and lower blooms.

The **depth of field** is the range or distance within which the camera can focus (with acceptable sharpness) on objects when you are taking a picture.

TIP

Lower f-stop settings work great for taking portraits, such as baby pictures, when you want to really focus on the subject, yet have a soft effect in the background.

So, when you're using the aperture priority mode for your camera, you choose the f-stop aperture setting you want, and the camera chooses an appropriate shutter speed. The LCD display on the back of the camera will show the selected aperture value. Follow these steps to use aperture priority mode if it's offered on your camera:

1. Power up the camera.
2. Use the Mode button or dial to choose the aperture priority picture-taking mode, often designated by an **A** (or **AV** for Aperture Value on some cameras).
3. If you had to press the Mode button in Step 2, a menu of modes should appear on the camera's LCD. Press the appropriate arrow button on the rocker/controller button until you've selected the **A** or **AV** mode, and then press Set or OK.
4. Press the appropriate arrow button on the rocker/controller button until the LCD display indicates the desired aperture setting, as in **F5.6** or **f/5.6**.
5. Compose and shoot the picture.

USING BRACKETING TO EXPLORE YOUR EXPOSURE OPTIONS

Having the LCD screen to preview what a digital camera will shoot certainly gives today's camera users a huge advantage over photographers using film cameras. After all, if we're using the LCD to compose our pictures, we see a good indication of how the final image will look as we take it.

Proficient photographers have long used a simple technique to work around the fact that they're flying a bit blind without a live picture preview. The technique is called *exposure bracketing*. To use exposure bracketing, simply take multiple shots of a subject at three or more similar f-stop settings (f/4, f/5.6, and f/8, for example) or three or more consecutive shutter speeds. This simple technique produces images with a variety of exposures so you can choose the image you prefer.

Figure 3.8 illustrates three bracketed exposures. The left image, shot at f/2, clearly is overexposed, with washed-out colors. The second and third shots, taken at f/5.6 and f/8, are quite similar. If you prefer high contrast, then you might prefer the third shot. However, others might like the more balanced tones in the statue's face in the second shot. With bracketing, you'll learn how taking control of the aperture can help you create more nuanced pictures.

FIGURE 3.8 Pictures taken with exposure bracketing at f/2, f/5.6, and f/8.

Controlling Shutter Speed

The other mode you can use to work with image quality is shutter priority mode. In shutter priority mode, you specify how long the shutter stays open after you press the shutter button, and the camera sets the aperture size automatically. Shutter speeds are expressed in seconds and fractions of sections, with a 1/60 shutter speed meaning that the shutter will be open for one-sixtieth of a second.

The longer the shutter stays open, the more light that can pass through the aperture and strike the camera sensor. So, for example, a 1/50 shutter speed exposes the image half as long as a 1/25 shutter speed. Even cameras in the lower part of the midrange offer a wide range of shutter speeds—from 1/1000 of a second to two seconds or so. When you have a slow shutter speed but are shooting a moving subject, the subject may be blurry as in Figure 3.9. In general, choose slower shutter speeds for static subjects. Choose faster shutter speeds for moving subjects. As with aperture priority mode, your camera may not compensate correctly for the selected shutter speed, so you may get a slightly overexposed image for slow shutter speeds, or an underexposed image for fast shutter speeds. As such, it's a good idea to try various shutter speed settings when you're shooting a particular subject.

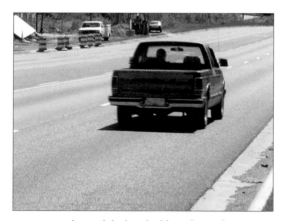

FIGURE 3.9 The truck looks a bit blurry here when compared to the background because the shutter speed used for the shot was too low.

Why would you opt to choose a shutter setting? Controlling the shutter speed is particularly good in two instances:

♦ **Shutter priority mode is best for capturing motion.** With a fast shutter speed, such as 1/1000, you can freeze a thousandth of a second in a picture, eliminating a lot of the blur that would appear in the image if it were shot at a lower shutter speed.

✦ **For some digital cameras, particularly those with a manual mode that enables you to choose both aperture and shutter settings, a slow shutter speed also enables you to expose an image properly when extremely low lighting conditions would otherwise prevent it.** With a shutter speed setting of a second or more, the shutter stays open long enough to let light strike the sensor for a lengthy period, enabling the exposure to accumulate to create the image.

CAUTION

If you want to use long exposure times, you should definitely use a tripod or place the camera on some other stationary surface. Otherwise, the jiggle from your unsteady hands will show up as blurring in the final image.

In shutter priority mode, the LCD display on the back of the camera will show the selected shutter speed. Follow these steps to use shutter priority mode, if it is available on your camera:

1. Power up the camera.
2. Use the Mode button or dial to choose the shutter priority picture-taking mode, often designated by an **S** (or **TV** for Time Value).
3. If you had to press the Mode button in Step 2, a menu of modes should appear on the camera's LCD. Press the appropriate arrow button on the rocker/controller button until you've selected the **S** or **TV** mode, and then press Set or OK.
4. Press the appropriate arrow button on the rocker/controller button until the LCD display indicates the desired shutter speed setting, as in **1/25** or **1/125**.
5. Compose and shoot the picture.

NOTE

Some digital cameras might not offer shutter priority mode, but they might offer another mode called something like "Long Time Exposure" to enable you to take pictures with longer shutter exposure times. Consult your camera's user manual to see whether your camera has such a feature.

Using Exposure Compensation

If your camera doesn't offer aperture priority and shutter priority modes (or even if it does), it might offer another option for overcoming the limitations of automatic (auto exposure) mode: exposure compensation. With *exposure compensation*, you can adjust exposure quickly to make a picture one or two steps lighter or darker in modes other than aperture priority or shutter priority modes. This helps you adjust for situations such as backlighting or heavy outdoor lighting on the fly, without having to change the flash or experiment with aperture or shutter priority modes.

Follow these steps to work with exposure compensation:

1. Power up the camera and choose a picture-taking mode.
2. If necessary, press the Menu button on your camera. (This step isn't necessary for all cameras.)
3. Press the appropriate arrow buttons (either up/down or left/right) on the rocker/controller control to set the desired exposure compensation. On some cameras, you simply choose a value setting, and then press OK or Set to accept the change, at which time you can check the image preview in the LCD. For other cameras, you simply watch the picture preview and press the arrow buttons until the picture preview looks as light or dark as you want. (Exposure compensation values are identified with EV, so an **EV** indicator may appear on the LCD once you start changing the exposure compensation.)
4. Compose and shoot the picture.

> **NOTE**
>
> Some digital cameras also offer an automatic exposure bracketing feature. To learn more about this feature for your camera, consult the camera's user manual.

Using Digital Zoom

As noted in Chapter 1, with optical zoom, your camera's lens telescopes to change the focal length, which magnifies or zooms the image. Digital cameras also use digital zoom, in which the camera mathematically interpolates data to increase the image size. Using the digital zoom requires two overall steps for many digital cameras—making sure the digital zoom feature is turned on, and then knowing how to kick in the digital zoom feature when you are zooming.

To turn on the digital zoom feature for a digital camera that requires it:

1. Power up the camera.
2. Press the Menu button, typically found on the back of the camera.
3. Press the down arrow on the rocker/controller button (also on the back of the camera) to scroll down to the setting category that includes the zoom function. (If your camera doesn't use setting categories, skip to Step 5.)
4. Press the OK button (often found in the center of the rocker/controller button) or the right arrow on the rocker/controller button. The available settings will be listed, like the ones shown in Figure 3.10.
5. Press the down arrow button on the rocker/controller button to scroll down to the Digital Zoom setting.
6. Press the OK button or the Set button.
7. If a submenu appears, use the down arrow and OK/Set to choose the On setting.

FIGURE 3.10 For some cameras, you must turn on the digital zoom feature.

When you want to use the digital zoom feature, follow these steps:

1. Choose a picture-taking mode and other settings.
2. Press the zoom control thumb toward the T (tight or telephoto) to zoom in on the subject, watching the LCD as you zoom.
3. When the zooming stops, release the zoom control thumb briefly, and then press it again. (On some cameras, you can simply keep holding the zoom control toward T.) The LCD preview will jump to the digital zoom, and an indicator such as **2x** will typically appear on the LCD.
4. Finish composing and shooting the picture.

Using Special Modes for Special Shots

In this chapter:

- ◆ Getting a close-up shot
- ◆ Shooting a landscape
- ◆ Going wide with a panorama
- ◆ Using modes for shooting at night or in low light
- ◆ Catching the action with fast shooting modes
- ◆ Getting in on the picture with a self timer

he last chapter explained how you can use manual settings, if offered by your camera, to get better pictures in different lighting conditions. This chapter takes a look at some automatic modes and features that your camera might offer instead of or in addition to the aperture priority mode and other features you just learned about.

This chapter teaches you how to use modes for taking close-up, landscape, and panorama pictures. In addition, you will see how to shoot in low light, use modes for shooting motion, and set a self timer so you can jump into the picture.

Taking a Close-Up

An extreme close-up picture of a subject can bring out fascinating detail, such as the veins in a flower petal or the red hourglass on a black widow's belly. A close-up can help you appreciate the shape of a woman's eyebrow or the perfect arrangement of hairs on a dog's face.

Most digital cameras offer either a *close-up* or *macro* mode for taking pictures of subjects close to the camera. Depending on the capabilities of your camera and its optical and digital zoom, the close-up or macro mode might enable you to capture subjects that are as close as 2.5 inches (or with some cameras, even closer) from the camera. Often, images shot in the macro or close-up mode will have a shallow depth of field, as shown in Figure 4.1, so the subject really "pops" in the picture.

The *macro* or *close-up* modes are lens focus modes that enable you to get very close to a subject to take a picture. The macro mode usually yields highly dramatic shots.

FIGURE 4.1 A camera's macro or close-up mode yields dramatic pictures.

Follow these steps when you want to use the close-up or macro mode to take a picture of a close-up subject:

1. Power up the camera, if that's a separate action for your camera.
2. Move the Mode dial to the close-up mode position.
   OR
   Press the focus control button as many times as needed to display the icon for the macro focus mode in the LCD preview and/or indicator display.

> **TIP**
>
> Most cameras identify either the close-up mode or the macro mode with a tulip icon.

3. Use the LCD preview to compose the picture, zooming as needed.
4. Press the shutter button about halfway down until the camera beeps and you see the image come into focus on the LCD. For some cameras, you have to choose the widest angle, and then move the camera back and forth to help it achieve sharp focus. In addition, your camera may signal accurate focus by changing the color of the tulip on the LCD preview.
5. Press and hold the shutter button for about a second to take the picture.

> **TIP**
>
> In most cases, your camera will turn off the flash automatically if you choose the close-up mode. You will have to turn the flash back on if it is needed. When you're working with a camera that treats the macro mode as a focus mode rather than a picture-taking mode, it might have limits for the aperture settings you can use (in aperture priority mode) along with macro mode.

WHAT ABOUT PORTRAITS?

Some digital cameras offer an additional mode called *portrait mode* that you can use to take a picture of a subject that's a normal distance (several feet away) from you. Like a low (large or wide) aperture setting, this mode blurs the background to highlight the subject. In Figure 4.2, notice how the grass behind Rika is blurred, yet her face has strong focus and detail. (Shooting down at the subject can help enhance the effect.)

Most often, you'll use the portrait mode with human subjects and pets, but you also can have success using it to shoot plant and still-life subjects.

FIGURE 4.2 If your camera offers a portrait mode, you can use it to take pictures of subjects that are several feet away.

Using a Landscape Mode

Unlike the portrait mode, the landscape mode enables you to create pictures where everything from the foreground to the background is in focus. (Typically, the camera will achieve this by selecting a higher f-stop setting for a smaller aperture in this mode.) For example, in Figure 4.3, you can see that the dog in the foreground is focused, as is the tree in the distance that appears to be in the middle of the road. Generally, you should use the landscape mode outdoors in sunny conditions (otherwise, you might not see much difference from an automatic mode shot). Even though the camera will try to keep everything in focus, ideally the prime subject of the image should be about 50 feet away from you.

Follow these steps to take a picture in landscape mode:

1. Power up the camera, if that's a separate action for your camera.
2. Move the Mode dial to the Landscape mode position.
   OR
   Press the Mode button. A menu of modes should appear on the camera's LCD. Press the appropriate arrow button on the rocker/controller button until you've selected the landscape mode, and then press Set or OK.

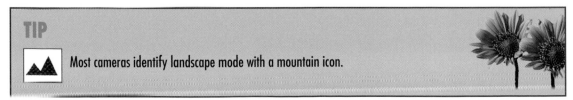

TIP

Most cameras identify landscape mode with a mountain icon.

3. Use the LCD preview to compose the picture, zooming as needed.
4. Press the shutter button about halfway down until the camera beeps and you see the image come into focus on the LCD.
5. Press and hold the shutter button for about a second, or until the camera signals that it has taken the picture.

TIP

Some cameras also offer an infinity focus mode to help the camera better focus on very distant objects.

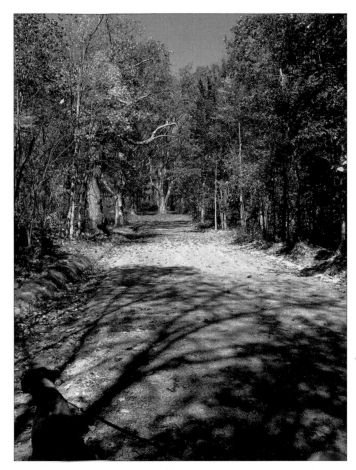

FIGURE 4.3 Landscape mode keeps everything in focus.

Shooting a Panorama

Some digital cameras offer a panorama recording mode. This mode enables you to take a sequence of images that you can combine to form a single wider image. Some cameras can combine the image for you on the camera LCD when you play back or preview the images.

To combine the individual shots into a finished panorama graphic, use an image editing program, such as Adobe Photoshop Elements 2.0. (Elements calls the feature for combining shots into a panorama "Photomerge.") Your cameras also may include software for stitching together panorama shots. For example, Figure 4.4 shows three images taken in panorama mode. The right end of the first image will overlap with the left end of the second one, and the right end of the second image will overlap the left end of the third one.

FIGURE 4.4 Three images shot in panorama mode, which will be combined into a finished panorama image.

Figure 4.5 shows the three images from Figure 4.4 overlapped to form a single image and saved as a new image file. (The ragged edges were left intentionally to show you how the three images were combined; you will probably prefer to crop your panorama images so they have straight edges.) The section called "Creating a Panorama or Collage" in Chapter 7, "Taking a Photo from Yawn to Wow," will explain how to create a photo panorama. For now, I'll show you how to shoot the images for a panorama with your camera.

FIGURE 4.5 This finished panorama combines the three images from Figure 4.4.

CAUTION

As you can see from the result in Figure 4.5, you have to be *really* steady with your hands to get the vertical alignment between shots right in panorama mode. Using a tripod to take your panorama shots will help eliminate this problem.

Follow these steps to take a picture in panorama mode:

1. Power up the camera, if that's a separate action for your camera.
2. Press the Mode button. A menu of modes should appear on the camera's LCD. Press the appropriate arrow button on the rocker/controller button until you've selected the panorama mode, and then press Set or OK.

③ Use the LCD preview to compose the first picture, zooming as needed.

④ Press the shutter button about halfway down until the camera beeps and you see the image come into focus on the LCD.

⑤ Press and hold the shutter button for about a second to take the picture.

⑥ Still viewing the LCD, point the camera a bit further to the right. The left side of the LCD will show a strip representing the right edge of the previous photo; try to line up the preview of the current photo with the information from the last photo.

⑦ Press and hold the shutter button to take the picture.

⑧ Repeat Steps 6 and 7 to take additional shots for the panorama as desired.

4

NOTE

For most digital cameras, when you turn the camera off and then back on, it reverts to the automatic mode and other default settings for the camera (such as the default flash setting).

Taking a Shot in Low Light

Taking good photos in nighttime lighting conditions has always been a challenge. Your digital camera might help with this problem by offering a night scene mode or a night mode for taking pictures. Of course, there's less light to be captured at night. Even indoor settings with low lighting can be extremely hard to capture. The night scene or night mode works by keeping the shutter open longer to allow more light to accumulate for the exposure, as if you had chosen a slow shutter speed in shutter priority mode. The camera also will likely choose a wider aperture setting. Of course, photos taken in the night mode won't look like they were taken in the daytime. Usually, they will give you a pleasing, glowing view of the scene, like the example (taken at a resort in Jamaica) in Figure 4.6.

TIP

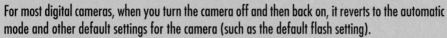

For dim (an overcast day) but not low (night) lighting conditions, you might want to use the *white balance* feature (if it's available) for your camera to correct the image tone. With a white balance setting, you can automatically or manually brighten the image so that the whitest tone is true white and other tones are lightened accordingly. Consult your camera's user manual to see how to use its white balance settings.

FIGURE 4.6 A shot taken with night scene mode.

Follow these steps when you want to use the night scene or night mode to take a picture under low evening or night lighting conditions:

1. Power up the camera, if that's a separate action for your camera.
2. Move the Mode dial to the night mode position.
   OR
   Press the Mode button. A menu of modes should appear on the camera's LCD. Press the appropriate arrow button on the rocker/controller button until you've selected the night scene mode, and then press Set or OK.

TIP

 Most cameras identify the night scene or night mode with an icon that has a person with a star (shown here) or a star and a moon.

---

3. Use the LCD preview to compose the picture, zooming as needed.
4. Press the shutter button about halfway down until the camera beeps and you see the image come into focus on the LCD.
5. Press and hold the shutter button for about a second to take the picture.

CAUTION

Because night scene or night mode keeps the shutter open longer, any shaking will show up as blurring in the image. Using a tripod with this mode gives better results. Keep in mind that with night scene or night mode, as with a number of other focus and picture-taking modes, you can add flash to improve the picture results. However, flash may not reach subjects that are too distant from the camera.

Shooting Motion

We've all shot blurry pictures with our film cameras. You have to be using a fast shutter speed to be able to freeze a moving subject so it looks still in the image, rather than like a big blur. Most digital cameras now offer one or more different modes for freezing motion.

Most digital cameras offer a mode called something like sport mode to enable you to snap a single image when the subject is in motion. The camera senses the lighting conditions and motion and sets an accordingly fast shutter speed for you. Other digital cameras offer burst mode (also called continuous mode), in which the camera automatically takes multiple consecutive shots (such as taking 3 shots per second) to freeze motion. This mode enables the photographer to catch unanticipated nuances in the action. Figure 4.7 shows a series of images shot in burst mode. Even though the car is moving, the images aren't blurry.

FIGURE 4.7 Shot in burst mode, these shots show the car moving out of the picture frame.

Follow these steps when you want to use a motion mode to take a picture of a moving subject:

1. Power up the camera, if that's a separate action for your camera.
2. Move the Mode dial to the sport (or comparable) mode position.
   OR
   Press the Menu button, usually found on the back of the camera. Use the appropriate arrow buttons on the rocker/controller button, as well as the Set or OK button, to navigate through the camera's menu system (view it on the LCD) and choose the burst or continuous drive or shutter mode.
3. Use the LCD preview to compose the picture, zooming as needed.
4. Press the shutter button about halfway down until the camera beeps and you see the image come into focus on the LCD.
5. Press and hold the shutter button to take the picture.

Using a Self-Timer

Most people don't want to miss out on being in the family portrait—even the family photo bug who's taking the picture. Most digital cameras offer a self-timer. With that feature, the photographer can compose the picture, press the shutter button, and then join the other photo subjects during a delay period (such as 2 or 10 seconds) before the camera actually takes the picture.

Follow these steps to use the self-timer feature of your digital camera:

1. Power up the camera, if that's a separate action for your camera.
2. Place the camera on a tripod or a flat, secure surface. Because you will not be holding the camera while you are taking the picture, the camera needs to be placed into position before you compose the shot.
3. Compose the shot using one of the still modes. (You typically can't use the self-timer for a motion shot.)
4. Press the Menu button, usually found on the back of the camera. Use the appropriate arrow buttons on the rocker/controller button, as well as the Set or OK button, to navigate through the camera's menu system (view it on the LCD) and enable the self-timer.

   OR

   Press the timer button on the camera (usually found on the top of the camera) repeatedly to select the desired time delay setting.
5. Press the shutter button about halfway down until the camera beeps and you see the image come into focus on the LCD.
6. Press and hold the shutter button for about a second, as if you were taking the picture. The camera should start beeping a countdown and/or displaying countdown numbers on the LCD. Some cameras also have a light that blinks to count down so that everyone in front of the camera can watch and be ready.
7. Join the other folks in the picture and say "cheese."

PART II

Working with Your Images

5

Transferring Images to Your Computer

In this chapter:

- ✦ Transferring images from a media card reader to your computer
- ✦ Connecting your camera to your PC via USB
- ✦ Using a camera dock to transfer pictures
- ✦ Making the transfer in Windows XP
- ✦ Printing images from the camera in Windows XP
- ✦ Viewing a slideshow of images from the camera in Windows XP

You're loving taking pictures with your digital camera. But wait! There's no more room on the camera's storage card. Once you've loaded up your camera's storage card with great shots, you need to offload them to your PC to make more room for even more photographic fun. What's more, once your pictures are on your PC, you can edit, print, and share your images online.

This chapter teaches you how to move pictures from your digital camera to your PC by a variety of methods, such as using a media card reader, a direct connection, or the docking device for your camera. You'll also see how to use Windows XP's built-in features to handle the transfer, print photos directly from your camera, or even view a slideshow of the images in the camera.

Working with a Digital Media Reader

If your digital camera doesn't include a dock for image transfers, you might want to purchase a digital media card reader that connects to your computer via a USB port. Although you could opt to simply connect your camera to the computer to transfer images, as described in the next section of this chapter, a media card reader offers convenience. Because the reader's always ready for you, you can simply take the card out of your camera and pop it into the card reader. There are numerous USB storage card readers for CompactFlash, Memory Stick, Smart Media, and Secure Digital storage cards. A number of card readers can read multiple types of media, and some even connect via a faster FireWire connection. Most readers work with either a Macintosh or a PC. If you plan to upload digital photos frequently, readers present a convenient, cheap ($20–40 for a basic reader), and attractive alternative to connecting your camera repeatedly.

To make the connection with a digital media card reader, follow these steps:

1 Install the media card reader as directed in its user manual. Typically, this involves connecting the reader to the USB port, as shown in Figure 5.1, and running the installation software provided with the device under Windows (especially if you're using a version of the Windows operating system prior to Windows XP).

2 Insert a storage card into the reader, as shown in Figure 5.1. The media reader slots or the contents of the storage card will mount as a disk in Windows, either on the desktop or in My Computer. *See Page 68 caution*

FIGURE 5.1 Media card readers attach to the USB port.

NOTE

If you're using Windows XP, your computer might prompt you to specify how to handle the photos at this point. If that happens, skip ahead to the section of this chapter called "Transferring the Images in Windows XP." If you're using a Macintosh with its latest operating system OS X, you will be prompted to transfer images into iPhoto.

❸ Double-click on the disk icon to open a folder for the camera storage card, and then navigate to the folder that holds the images to view (see Figure 5.2). For most cameras, you have to open a folder called DCIM to find the image files or the subfolders that hold the image files.

TIP

Some cameras create a subfolder for each date on which you take pictures to hold the pictures shot on that date.

❹ Once you've opened a folder that holds the pictures to move or copy to your PC, you can handle the move or copy operation just as you would for any other file (see Figure 5.3). First, select the picture file(s) to move or copy to your PC.

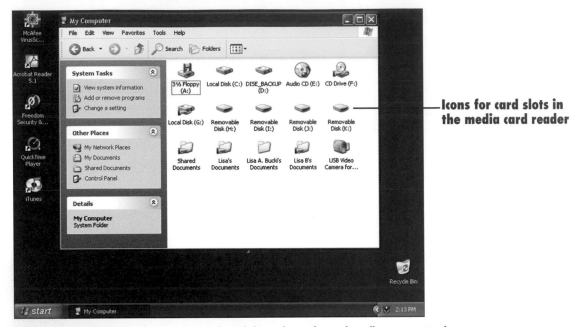

Icons for card slots in the media card reader

FIGURE 5.2 An icon for the media card or each card slot in the media reader will appear in Windows.

Selected picture

FIGURE 5.3 Once you're viewing your pictures in a Windows folder, you can move or copy them just like any other file.

66 Transferring Images to Your Computer

⑤ Choose Edit, Cut (to move the picture) or Edit, Copy (to copy the picture). Windows will copy the picture file(s) to the Clipboard in the system's memory.

5

⑥ Use Windows to navigate to the folder on your hard disk where you want to store the photos.
⑦ Choose Edit, Paste (see Figure 5.4). The specified digital picture file(s) will be placed in the destination folder.

⑧ After you finish transferring photos, eject the storage card by dragging its disk icon to the Recycle Bin (Trash on a Mac) if required by your reader. You must follow this step if working on a Mac.
⑨ Remove the storage card from the reader and place it back in the camera.

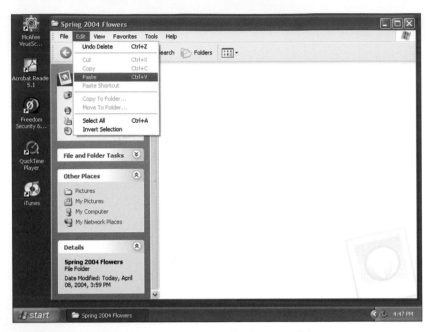

FIGURE 5.4 Paste the copied or cut pictures into the destination folder.

CAUTION

The media reader is like a disk drive. Never remove the storage card when the drive reading light is on; otherwise, you might damage the images. The same goes for your camera. If the memory or storage light is on, do not remove the card from the camera.

Working with a USB Connection

If you don't mind a few extra minutes of work each time you need to transfer digital photos, you can attach your camera directly to your computer using the cable provided with the camera. Many manufacturers include a serial cable, but because that type of connection is dramatically slower, you'll want to use the USB cable that came with your camera and transfer pictures via USB instead.

Follow this process to set up your camera to transfer images to your computer via USB:

1. Install the camera driver software under Windows, as directed by the camera's user manual. This software will ensure that Windows can recognize your camera, although this step might not be necessary under Windows XP.
2. Attach the camera's AC adapter, if any, and plug it into a power receptacle. This step conserves battery power and ensures the camera will have power to complete the entire transfer operation.
3. Plug the larger end of the USB cable into a USB port on your computer.
4. Open the door that covers the camera's USB port on the side of the camera.
5. Plug the smaller end of the USB cable into the port on the side of the camera.
6. Turn the camera's mode/power/function switch to the PLAY (playback), ON, or another image transfer position as specified in the camera's user manual.
7. At this point, you can transfer the images using one of the following methods:
   + If you're working with a Windows version prior to Windows XP and your camera mounts as a disk icon, follow Steps 3 through 7 in the earlier "Working with a Digital Media Reader" section to move the images from the camera's storage card to the desired folder.

   + If your camera's driver software included special software for transferring images, follow the onscreen prompts (and consult the camera's user manual as needed) to complete the transfer.
   + If you're working with Windows XP and the dialog box shown in Figure 5.5 asks you what Windows should do with the pictures, follow the steps in the "Transferring Images in Windows XP" section to move the images from the camera to the computer.
8. When you've finished transferring images, power down the camera, disconnect the USB and power source, and close the door on the side of the camera.

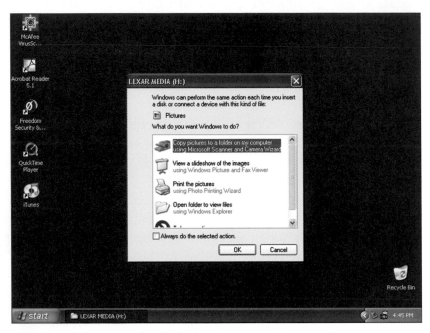

FIGURE 5.5 Windows XP can handle the digital image transfer process for you.

Working with a Camera Dock

Some cameras provide a dock to increase convenience in transferring photos from the camera to the printer. Further, a dock will typically recharge any battery pack that was included with the camera. Typically, you can mark the images that you want to transfer on the camera, seat the camera in the dock, and press a single button to initiate the transfer.

Before you start using the dock, follow these steps to properly install and connect it to your computer, using the dock's user's guide to provide specific information about the setup procedure for your dock:

1. Install the software and/or drivers that came with the dock, as directed in its user's guide.
2. If your dock requires a special insert for use with your digital camera, install that insert. The insert will ensure that your camera model can connect securely with the dock.
3. Connect the dock to the USB port on the computer. You may need to use the same USB cable that came with your digital camera, or purchase a separate USB cable for use with the dock.
4. Attach the dock's AC adapter and plug it into a power receptacle. This will power on the dock, so that it's ready to transfer pictures. (Also press the On button for the dock, if needed.)

Once you've set up the dock as specified, use these steps to use the dock to transfer images from the camera to your PC:

1. Power down the camera and put on its lens cap. (Only leave the camera on if required by your dock.)
2. Open the sliding door that protects the camera dock connector, as shown in Figure 5.6.
3. Seat the camera in the dock, as shown in Figure 5.7.

FIGURE 5.6 A sliding door protects the camera's dock connector. Open this door before docking the camera.

FIGURE 5.7 A docked camera.

④ Press the dock's transfer or move button. The dock will read the photo data from the camera and one of two things will happen:

✦ If your camera mounts as a disk icon, follow Steps 3 through 7 in the earlier "Working with a Digital Media Reader" section to move the images from the camera's storage card to the desired folder.

✦ If your dock's and camera's software included special software for transferring images, follow the onscreen prompts (and consult the dock's and camera's user manuals as needed) to complete the transfer.

CAUTION

To use the dock to charge a rechargeable battery pack, you typically make sure that the dock is powered on, and then seat the camera in the dock (without turning the camera on).

Transferring the Images in Windows XP

Windows XP recognizes many current digital camera models, and it comes with built-in capabilities for managing digital images. You can use XP's Microsoft Scanner and Camera Wizard to transfer images from your digital camera to a folder on your system's hard disk. The Scanner and Camera Wizard shows a preview of every image on the camera's storage card, no matter what subfolder holds the image. This eliminates the need to navigate numerous folders to access the images that you want to transfer.

Follow these steps to use the Microsoft Scanner and Camera Wizard to transfer pictures from your camera to your computer's hard disk:

❶ Connect the camera for transfer as described in the "Working with a USB Connection" section.

❷ When the dialog box shown in Figure 5.5 appears, leave the Copy Pictures to a Folder on My Computer Using Microsoft Scanner and Camera Wizard choice selected, and then click on OK. The wizard will read the storage card in your camera, and then display its Welcome screen.

❸ After reading the Welcome information, click on Next. The Choose Pictures to Copy screen of the wizard will appear (see Figure 5.8).

❹ If you want to copy only selected photos, click on the Clear All choice at the lower-right corner of the picture preview, and then continue to Step 5. Otherwise, skip this step and go on to Step 6.

❺ Click to place a check in the check box of each photo you want to transfer.

The wizard will transfer checked photos

FIGURE 5.8 Click to place a check mark beside each picture to transfer.

TIP

If a photo's image appears to be lying on its side, click on the image preview, and then click on the Rotate Clockwise or Rotate Counterclockwise button.

CAUTION

Your digital camera also stores a smaller preview version of each image you shoot. These previews will appear in the Scanner and Camera Wizard. If your camera groups those preview images in a preview folder, a preview heading will appear in the list of image previews to help you avoid selecting those images. Otherwise, to make sure you're getting the highest-resolution version of any shot, click on the image, and then click on the Properties button.

6. Click on Next. The Picture Name and Destination screen of the wizard will appear.

7. Enter a name for the group of pictures in the Type a Name for This Group of Pictures text box. The wizard will use the group name you entered to rename the photos in sequence. For example, if you enter Balboa Park, as shown here, the transferred photos will be renamed Balboa Park 001, Balboa Park 002, and so on. The wizard thus provides an automated method to replace the numeric file names assigned by the camera with more meaningful names.

8. Use the Browse button beside the Choose a Place to Save This Group of Pictures option to open the Browse for Folder dialog box, which you can then use to choose the folder on your hard disk where the wizard will save the pictures (see Figure 5.9).

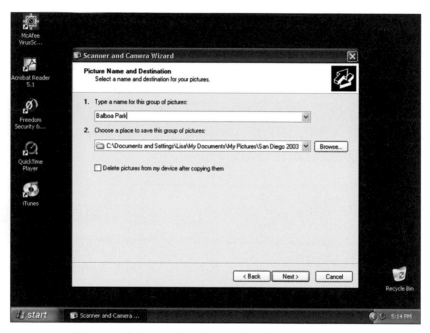

FIGURE 5.9 Tell the wizard where to place the transferred pictures.

9. (Optional) If you want the wizard to delete the pictures from the camera after they've been transferred to your computer, click to place a check in the Delete Pictures from my Device after Copying Them check box.

10. Click on Next. The Copying Pictures screen of the wizard will inform you as the copy operation progresses and then finishes. Then, the Other Options screen will appear to ask whether you want to publish the pictures to a Web site or order prints online.

11. Leave Nothing. I'm Finished Working with These Pictures selected, and click on Next. The final screen of the wizard will appear.

12. Click Finish. The wizard will close, and a folder window for the folder holding the transferred images will appear as shown in Figure 5.10.

FIGURE 5.10 Finish the wizard and look at your pictures.

Printing a Batch of Images Directly from the Camera in Windows XP

When you connect your camera under Windows XP, you also have the option to use the Photo Printing Wizard to print images directly from the camera without copying them to the hard disk. This feature saves you time when you want to share a picture with someone, pronto. Chapter 9, "Printing Your Photos," will provide a more detailed discussion of how to print your pictures, but you can follow these steps to get quick printouts from the camera with Windows XP:

1. Connect the camera for transfer as described in the "Working with a USB Connection" section earlier in this chapter.
2. When the dialog box shown in Figure 5.5 appears, click on Print the Pictures in the list of choices, and then click on OK. The wizard will read the storage card in your camera, and then display the Photo Printing Wizard Welcome screen.
3. Click on Next. The Picture Selection screen of the wizard will appear.

④ If you want to print only selected photos, click on the Clear All button at the lower-right corner of the picture preview, and then continue to Step 5. Otherwise, skip this step and go on to Step 6.

⑤ Click to place a check in the check box for each photo you want to print (see Figure 5.11).

Also check the photos to print

FIGURE 5.11 Click to place a check mark beside each picture to print.

⑥ Click on Next. The Printing Options screen of the wizard will appear.

⑦ Choose the printer to use from the What Printer Do You Want to Use? drop-down list (see Figure 5.12).

⑧ (Optional) If you think you need to change the print settings, such as ink saturation, for the selected printer, click on the Printing Preferences button, change the desired settings, and return to the Photo Printing Wizard.

⑨ Click on Next. The Layout Selection wizard screen will appear (see Figure 5.13).

⑩ Scroll down the list of available layouts and click on the layout you want to use to print the photos. The Print Preview area at the right will show you what the selected layout looks like. Note that when you choose a layout in which multiple images are on a page, the wizard will automatically include multiple different images per page rather than repeating a single image, although you can override this setting by changing the Number of Times to Use Each Picture value.

⑪ Click on Next. The wizard will send the images to the printer and display its completion screen when it finishes.

⑫ Click on Finish to close the Photo Printing Wizard.

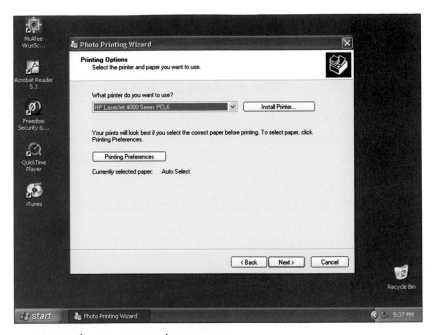

FIGURE 5.12 Choose a printer and print settings.

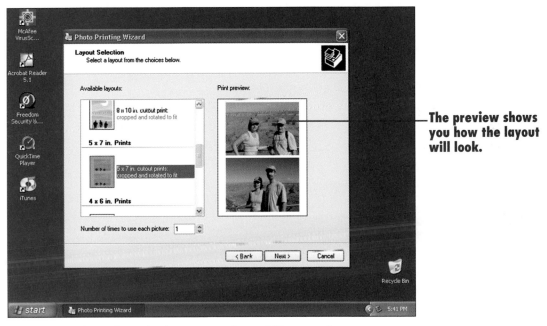

The preview shows you how the layout will look.

FIGURE 5.13 Click on a layout for the printout in the Available Layouts list.

Viewing a Slideshow of Images in Windows XP

If you're having a great party and you want to show your guests all the incriminating photos you've just taken, you can connect your camera to your computer and show a slideshow from the camera in Windows XP. Don't forget the popcorn when you follow these steps:

❶ Connect the camera for transfer, as described in the "Working with a USB Connection" section earlier in this chapter.

> When you run a *slideshow*, Windows displays one image after another onscreen at full-screen size.

❷ When the dialog box shown in Figure 5.5 appears, click on View a Slideshow of the Images in the list of choices, and then click on OK. The wizard will read the storage card in your camera, and then start displaying your photos onscreen.

Slideshow controls

FIGURE 5.14 Wiggle the mouse, and then use the controls that appear in the upper-right corner of the screen to control playback.

③ The images will be displayed in full-screen size, so if you want to move between images, wiggle the mouse button. Control buttons will appear in the upper-right corner of the screen. From left to right, the buttons start, pause, back up, jump forward, and exit the slideshow, respectively.

CAN I GET DIGITAL VERSIONS OF MY OLD PHOTOS OR NEGATIVES?

Most of us have decades' worth of photos taken with a traditional film camera sitting around the house. If you want to transform those images into a catalog of digital photos, you can do so. (Of course, when you're having newly-shot film processed, most photo processors give you the option of also receiving digital copies of your image files on CD.) The number of old photos or negatives that you convert and the method you choose to do so will depend on how much time and money you want to invest, but you do have a few options.

✦ Scan your photos yourself. Today's flatbed scanners feature reasonable prices ($100–300) and high-quality resolutions. Be sure to buy a scanner with 36-bit resolution or better. Some scanners offer the option of purchasing a sheet feeder, but those might not work well with smaller photos and may actually damage them.

✦ If you have 35mm slides and negatives to scan, check with your local camera shop or specialty photo-processing shop. Film and negative scanners might be out of your price range, but chances are your local camera or specialty-photo processing shop already has the expensive film scanner needed. These services typically can supply you with scans in a variety of resolutions and sizes.

✦ Find an online resource to scan your photos, slides, or negatives to PhotoCD or other format. These services might take a little longer and you will have to pay shipping costs, but they might be better equipped to handle a large number of scans, and they might give you more competitive pricing. Check out Advanced Digital Imaging at http://www.adiweb.com or Boston Photo at http://www.bostonphoto.com, both of which scan a variety of originals.

5

Improving Photos with Image Editing Software

In this chapter:

- ✦ Finding image editing software
- ✦ Rotating a photo to the proper orientation and cropping to eliminate unwanted areas
- ✦ Fixing red-eye in a picture
- ✦ Bringing out detail with fill lighting
- ✦ Using softening and sharpening tools
- ✦ Fixing spots and scratches
- ✦ Making corrections to the image tone and color

When you are working with digital images, your ability to be creative doesn't stop after you press the shutter. Using even a relatively inexpensive image editing program, you can correct problems with an image. For example, you can brighten an image taken in overcast outdoor conditions. Even better, you can enhance an image to make it more like a work of art than a snapshot.

This chapter teaches you how to use basic image editing tools to make photo corrections, such as rotating and cropping a picture or eliminating red-eye. You'll see how to use a fill lighting feature if it is offered by your image editing software, along with how to use other tools to soften or sharpen an image, fill in spots or scratches, or even work with image tone and color.

Finding the Right Image Editing Program

With film photography, a photographer has some control over image quality and cropping during the printing process in the darkroom. I say "some control" because darkroom workers can only do a small fraction of what's possible today with digital image editing software.

Even basic image editing programs, such as Adobe Photoshop Elements 2.0 or Jasc Paint Shop Pro 8, enable you to crop, resize, color correct, add text, and apply special filters or effects to images. They also enable you to perform specialized tasks, such as creating a Web photo gallery or merging images into a collage or panorama. Basic programs also typically can import images directly from your camera and print a variety of layouts, such as a picture package (a single-page layout of an image in various standard photo print sizes). Finally these programs offer tools for removing red-eye, fixing scratches or speckles on an image, or adding text or drawn elements to an image. Pro image editing programs typically add to the features offered in the small fries, giving you more detailed tools for making corrections, as well as tools for preparing images for professional publication.

Most hobby users will do quite well with a basic, less expensive image editing program. That being said, Table 6.1 also lists the pro-level programs so you can compare for yourself. These software publishers offer great details about each product on the Web, so the table includes the publisher Web site for each program. Go to the URL in the table below for up-to-date pricing. You also can download and install free trial versions of many of the programs so you can compare them head to head and choose the program that best suits your needs. (Be aware that trial versions often expire after a certain period or add watermark information to any image you save as an incentive to buy the program.)

TABLE 6.1 Image Editing Software

Software Name	URL
Less Expensive	
Adobe Photoshop Elements 2.0	http://www.adobe.com/products/photoshopel
CorelDRAW Essentials 2	http://www.corel.com, click on More Products link
Jasc Paint Shop Pro 8.0	http://www.jasc.com/products/paintshoppro
Professional	
Adobe Photoshop CS	http://www.adobe.com/products/photoshop
CorelDRAW Graphics Suite 12	http://www.corel.com, click on CorelDRAW Graphics Suite link
Microsoft Digital Image Pro 9	http://www.microsoft.com/products/imaging/products

6

TIP

Some photo album or catalog programs offer basic editing capabilities, such as the ability to remove red-eye. If you only want to perform the bare minimum of photo edits, but you also want to be able to better organize your digital images, consider one of those programs instead. See Chapter 8, "Managing Your Photo Library," for more information on photo album software.

Rotating a Picture and Cropping Out the Junk

Beginning photographers sometimes have the most trouble with something that seems simple—composing the picture. If you have a relative who cuts people's heads off in every picture, you know what I mean.

If the subject of a picture is tall, you will probably need to rotate the camera by 90 degrees to be able to zoom in as far as you want to take the picture. That will give you a digital image that appears to be lying on its side. When you transfer the image to your computer, you will need to rotate the image to work with it in its proper orientation. In other instances, beginners might tend to play it safe and not zoom in close enough on the subject. Or, you might be prevented from zooming in or getting closer due to the picture-taking circumstances.

NOTE

This book can't begin to give exact steps for performing every operation in every program. The overview steps presented provide you with clues as to how to get started in a program and identify the commands and features you should look for in a program when you want to solve a particular problem with an image.

You can use image editing software to correct these issues in a flash. Follow these steps to rotate and crop an image:

❶ Open the image to edit in the image editing software.

CAUTION

Although image editing programs typically offer you the opportunity to undo several changes, it's a good practice to keep a copy of the original image without changes. You can always make additional copies of the original image to try different edits and effects. Always follow this practice if the original images are TIFF files, because converting an image to the JPEG format applies compression that can't be removed.

2 Choose the command for rotating the image in the proper direction. For example, Figure 6.1 shows the rotation choices in Adobe Photoshop Elements 2.0, such as the 90° Right command on the Image, Rotate submenu.

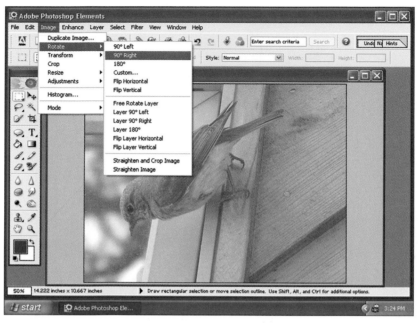

FIGURE 6.1 When an image has the wrong orientation and appears to be lying on its side, rotate it.

3 To crop an image, choose the crop tool in the software. When you move the mouse pointer over the image, you'll see that the mouse pointer has changed to a special crop pointer that looks like two overlapping corners.

4 Drag diagonally on the image to specify the area to crop, as shown in Figure 6.2. Any content outside the dashed selection marquee will be removed from the image when you apply the crop.

5 Adjust the crop zone as needed by dragging any of the square handles that appear around the selection marquee after you release the mouse button.

6 Click on the Apply or Commit button in the software toolbar to apply the crop. Figure 6.3 shows the image of the female bluebird after both rotating and cropping.

—Crop pointer

FIGURE 6.2 Cropping an image eliminates unwanted photo content.

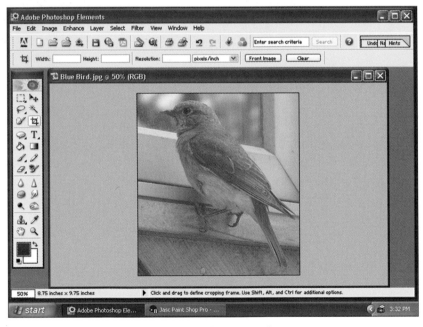

FIGURE 6.3 This image has been both rotated and cropped.

Eliminating Red-Eye

As you learned in the discussion of flash modes in Chapter 3, most digital cameras include a flash mode called red-eye or red-eye reduction that's designed to prevent the red-eye effect in photos taken with a flash. (Red-eye occurs in human and animal subjects when the flash bounces off the subject's retina and produces a red or green glow in one or both eyes.) If you failed to use the red-eye flash mode and you have an otherwise great image that you'd like to save, don't worry. Most image editing programs now include a special tool or feature for fixing red-eye.

Generally speaking, the red-eye tool will work in one of two ways after you've opened the image to correct:

◆ In some programs, such as Photoshop Elements, you click on a red-eye brush tool in the toolbox, and then click or drag on the area to correct in the image file (see Figure 6.4).

◆ In other programs, such as Paint Shop Pro, you choose the command for the red-eye removal tool from a menu (Adjust, Red-Eye Removal in the case of Paint Shop Pro), and then you use tools in a dialog box to apply the correction. Figure 6.5 shows the Red-Eye Removal dialog box in Paint Shop Pro. The red-eye area was selected in the image at the left, and the preview at the right shows how the image will look once the correction settings are applied.

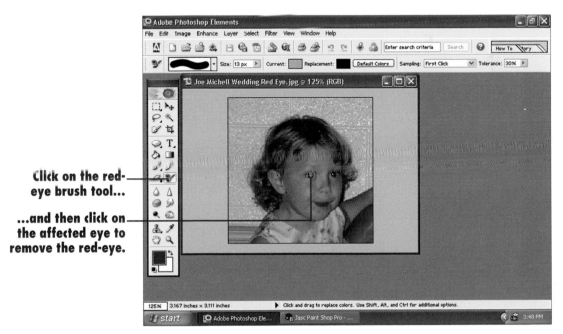

Click on the red-eye brush tool...

...and then click on the affected eye to remove the red-eye.

FIGURE 6.4 Eliminating red-eye using Photoshop Elements.

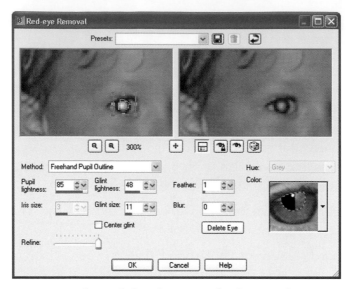

FIGURE 6.5 Working with the red-eye removal tool in Paint Shop Pro.

Adding Fill Lighting

Chapter 3 also introduced you to the concept of fill flash—using flash under very bright or high-contrast lighting conditions to ensure that details in the subject won't be drowned out in heavy shadows. If you transfer an image to your PC and realize it has areas that are too dark, you can work with the fill flash tool in your image editing software to correct the problem.

For example, consider the picture shown in Figure 6.6. The detail in my mom's face is virtually lost due to the heavy shadows caused by the bright sunlight. Take a look at how you can correct this image, again working with an open image in Photoshop Elements and Paint Shop Pro.

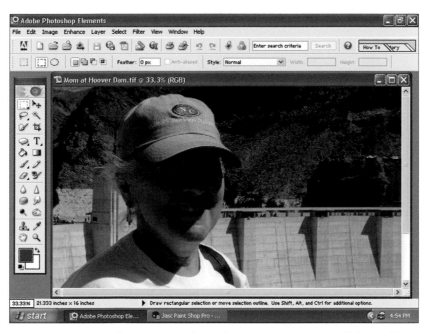

FIGURE 6.6 This shot, taken on a sunny day at the Hoover Dam, needs the help of a fill flash tool.

◆ In Photoshop Elements, select the portion of the image to correct. Choose Enhance, Adjust Lighting, Fill Flash. An Adjust Fill Flash dialog box will appear. As illustrated in Figure 6.7, drag the dialog box controls until the image's appearance improves as desired. If you compare the image in Figure 6.7 to the original in Figure 6.6, you can see that the fill flash adjustment has revealed much of the detail in Mom's face; you can even see her eyes behind her glasses. When you are satisfied with the changes, click on OK.

◆ Paint Shop Pro doesn't offer a specific tool for applying a fill flash effect. However, its One Step Photo Fix feature does a pretty good job of adding apparent light to bring out the detail in darker areas of a photo, among other corrections. To apply this feature, click on the Enhance Photo button on the Photo toolbar, and then click on One Step Photo Fix.

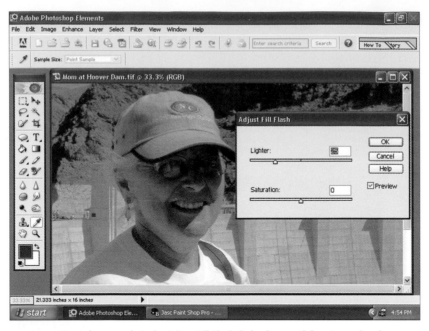

FIGURE 6.7 Drag the controls in the Adjust Fill Flash dialog box until the picture details emerge.

TIP

You also can use the dodge tool in an image editing program to lighten only selected areas in an image. Choose the dodge tool from the toolbox, choose brush shape and other settings from the options bar that appears near the top of the program window, and then drag on the dark areas of the image to bring out the detail.

Making an Image Sharper or Softer

Image editing programs also offer tools for affecting the apparent focus of an image. You can sharpen all or part of an image to make its details more dramatic. On the other hand, you can soften all or part of an image to give it a prettier effect. You also can use softening to make subtle image corrections, such as softening facial blemishes or wrinkles to reduce their appearance, or softening to hide dust or small scratches in the image.

Your image editing software might offer one or more tools for applying sharpness or softness to an image. After you select an area of the image to sharpen or soften, look for a technique like this to make the desired improvement.

◆ In Paint Shop Pro, click on the Enhance Photo button on the Photo toolbar, and then click on Sharpen. Or, choose Adjust, Sharpness, Sharpen from the menu bar. Repeat this operation as many times as needed to achieve the desired image sharpness (see Figure 6.8).

FIGURE 6.8 The right version of this image was sharpened in Paint Shop Pro. The shape of the croc's head is more defined in the right image after sharpening.

◆ Both Paint Shop Pro and Photoshop Elements offer an Unsharp Mask tool. In Paint Shop Pro, choose Adjust, Sharpness, Unsharp Mask. In Photoshop Elements, choose Filter, Sharpen, Unsharp Mask. Adjust settings in the Unsharp Mask dialog box that appears, checking the preview to ensure that the image looks the way you want it to, and then click OK.

◆ In Paint Shop Pro, choose Adjust, Softness, Soften to soften a selection in an image. Or, use Adjust, Softness, Soften More to apply a greater amount of softness. The Adjust, Softness, Soft Focus command displays a dialog box that you can use to apply a dramatic amount of softness at once.

◆ In Photoshop Elements, use the commands on the Filter, Blur submenu to blur the image or a selection. For example, Figure 6.9 shows the Gaussian Blur filter applied to the selected flower at the right. It previously was as sharp as the flower on the left.

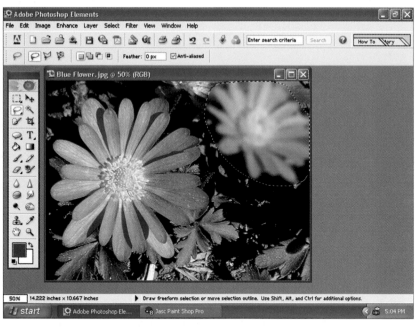

FIGURE 6.9 Gaussian blur was used to soften the selected flower at the right.

Removing Spots and Scratches

Occasionally, a digital image might appear to have spots or scratches resulting from a dirty lens or even foreign substances that were on the subject itself. Or, if you have a digital image that's actually a scan of an old family photo, the imperfections might be a result of actual droplets and cracks on the original photo's surface. While correcting imperfections like these used to be literally a matter of painting on a print, today you can use digital tools in your image editing program to make the correction.

Image editing programs offer a variety of different tools you can use to fix apparent "surface" imperfections in a digital image, including:

✦ **A scratch remover (Paint Shop Pro) or healing brush (Photoshop CS) tool.** Generally, you click the tool on the toolbar, set the brush settings if necessary, and then drag over the area to fix on the image. Figure 6.10 shows the scratch remover tool in Paint Shop Pro being used to fix a scratch in an image.

✦ **A patch or clone stamp tool.** With a tool like this, you sample or select an area that looks like you want the corrected area to look, typically by Alt+clicking (or using another mouse and keyboard combination) the area to sample, then click to apply the correction or patch over the scratch or spot.

✦ **Filters or commands for removing speckles, dust, scratches, and artifacts.** These filters help make automatic corrections over a wide area in the image so you don't have to paint or patch over errors one at a time (see Figure 6.11). When there's no selection in the image, the command or filter corrects the entire image. To limit the scope of correction, make a selection before invoking the command or filter.

JPEG images often have *artifacts*—imperfections in a JPEG image due to the fact that JPEG compression involves discarding image data. Artifacts include halos (color leakage beyond the edges of objects) and jagged or blocky-looking areas in the background.

FIGURE 6.10 Fixing an imperfection using the Paint Shop Pro scratch remover tool

FIGURE 6.11 Paint Shop Pro offers a variety of commands for correcting widespread image problems, such as speckles.

Correcting Image Tone and Color

The LCD preview on most digital cameras is still relatively small, so judging subtle factors, such as overall image tone, might be difficult. Luckily, image editing programs also offer a variety of commands for fixing the color in an image, either automatically or manually. Consult the Help system for your image editing program to learn about all of its capabilities. Here's a sampling of what's possible:

✦ Most programs offer commands for automatically adjusting color balance or color correction, brightness and contrast levels, or hue and saturation. Look for these commands on the Enhance or Adjust menus in your image editing program. Simply choose the command, and the image editing software automatically will examine and correct the photo.

✦ Look for a command like the Enhance, Quick Fix or Enhance, Adjust Color, Color Variations commands in Photoshop Elements. These commands display a window in which you can make a few simple choices to fix an image, as shown in Figure 6.12. In some cases, you can click on different previews to apply different color mixes to the image.

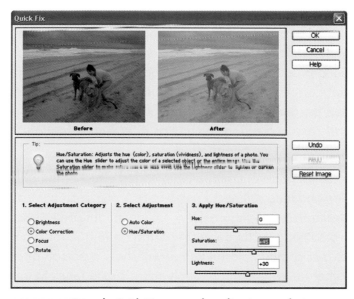

FIGURE 6.12 Using the Quick Fix command to adjust image color in Photoshop Elements.

◆ If you want the greatest level of control, choose one of the manual color correction commands via the Enhance or Adjust menu. Usually, the program will display a dialog box that enables you to specify precise tone or color corrections. For example, Figure 6.13 shows the Brightness/Contrast dialog box in Paint Shop Pro.

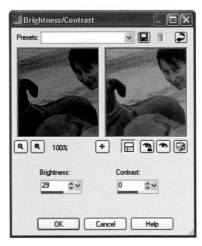

FIGURE 6.13 Most programs enable you to make manual color and tone corrections, such as specifying precise brightness and contrast settings.

When a photo has a lot of color and contrast problems, such as in the top photo in Figure 6.14, you will have to use multiple color and tone correction commands to improve the image. To produce the result in the bottom image, I used the Photoshop Elements Auto Color Correction command, manually adjusted brightness and contrast levels, and then used the dodge tool to further lighten the human and dog faces. You can use the tone and color correction commands in any combination. You can even repeat a single command to reapply its effect.

One final word: Personal preference and the intended effect of the photo weigh heavily when choosing color and tone settings. I personally prefer high contrast and fairly saturated colors, as illustrated in Figure 6.14. Others might prefer less contrast or color in their images for a softer look. If you're preparing an image for a newsletter or a printed sales piece, a crisp and colorful image will show a person or product more forcefully. On the other hand, you might apply more subtle tones to an image for a baby or engagement announcement card.

FIGURE 6.14 The top shot was taken on an overcast day, during the evening hours. Multiple color and tone corrections improved the bottom image.

6

Taking a Photo from Yawn to Wow

In this chapter:

- ✦ Applying a filter or effect
- ✦ Changing the image border
- ✦ Adding text to an image
- ✦ Achieving drama by converting to black-and-white or sepia
- ✦ Creating a panorama or collage

The last chapter started the discussion of using tools in image editing software to correct problems with image flash, exposure, and tone. This chapter moves on to introduce you to image editing tools for adding your own creative flair to an image rather than correcting problems. Using the tools and techniques presented here, you can convert even an average mug shot into an artistic portrait. Some photographer/artist professionals even use image editing software to prepare unique images offered in upscale art galleries.

Read on to explore artsy techniques, such as adding filters and special effects to an image, framing an image with a special border, and using text to enhance your creation. Next, try converting an image to black-and-white (grayscale) or another tone to achieve more drama or to age the picture. Finally, work with a merge or collage feature to create image panoramas and collages.

Applying Filters

Image editing programs offer filters (sometimes called *special effects*) to enable you to change the appearance of a digital image or selection within the image. For example, a filter can make an image look like it was painted with watercolors or drawn with charcoal. You can add ripple, twirl, texture, chrome, or many other effects to an image—it all depends on what filters or effects your image editing program offers. Even better, if you have an image that appears a little out of focus even though the subject matter is great, you can use filters to create attractive second takes on the original photo.

> **TIP**
>
> As noted in the last chapter, apply your changes to a copy of the original image file. That way, you can always make additional copies of the original image to try different edits and effects or return to the content of the original picture.

As for the techniques presented in the last chapter, the steps for applying a filter or effect (or performing the other operations described later) will vary somewhat depending on the image editing program you're using. Still, here's a useful overview of the steps for applying a filter to an image file:

① Open the image to edit in your image editing software.

② Select the area to which you want to apply the filter or effect.

CAUTION

Most image editing programs enable you to create multiple layers within the image file. If that's the case with the program you're using, be sure to also select the layer to which you want to apply the filter.

③ Choose the command for the desired filter. In Adobe Photoshop Elements, for example, click on the Filter menu, point to a filter category, and then click on the desired filter (as in Filter, Artistic, Paint Daubs). In Paint Shop Pro, click on the Effects menu, point to a filter category, and then click on the desired filter (as in Effects, Distortion Effects, Twirl).

④ In most cases, a dialog box like the one in Figure 7.1 will appear. Choose settings for the filter until the preview looks the way you want it to, and then click on OK to apply the filter.

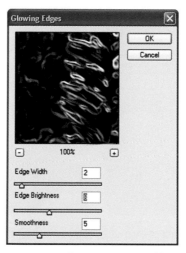

FIGURE 7.1 When you use many filters and effects, a dialog box appears to prompt you to choose specific filtering settings.

Figure 7.2 illustrates just some of the possibilities you can achieve by applying filters.

NOTE

You're not limited to applying one filter or effect. You can apply multiple filters and effects to achieve your own interesting combinations.

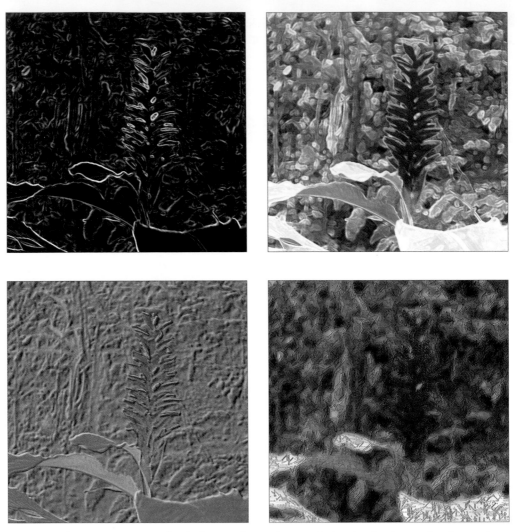

FIGURE 7.2 The same image treated with glowing edges and accented edges brushes (top row) and neon glow and straw bale texture effects (bottom row).

Adding Borders

If you don't like the look of plain white edges around your photos but you don't have a printer that can make borderless prints, many image editing programs offer you the ability to add a border or frame around an image. Borders and frames take one of three forms:

◆ An effect applied to the edges of the image to break it up into something other than a straight line, as shown in Figure 7.3. Figure 7.3 shows a spatter border.

A deckle edge border looks torn, mimicking a finish technique that used to be performed by photo labs, where the edges of the print would be cut in the deckle style.

◆ A decorative digital frame applied around the border of the image, as shown in Figure 7.4.

◆ A simple thick outline applied around the border of an image to better define the edge of the image.

FIGURE 7.3 The edges of this photo have a spattered border effect.

FIGURE 7.4 A fun digital frame can make an image more festive or decorative.

The steps for applying a border or frame to an image vary dramatically from program to program, so consult the Help system for your image editing program to learn the specific steps to add a border or frame. For example, in Photoshop Elements, you will have to use the Window, Effects command to open the Effects palette, choose Frames from the drop-down list in the upper-left corner of the palette to display only border effects (see Figure 7.5), and then click on the frame to apply it. In Paint Shop Pro, you choose Image, Picture Frame, and then work in the dialog box that appears to select and apply a frame. Paint Shop Pro also has an Image, Add Borders command to enable you to add a plain outline around the image.

> **TIP**
>
> Many online photo printing services also enable you to add borders to pictures before you have prints made. For more information on these services, see Chapter 11, "Transforming Photos into Keepsakes."

FIGURE 7.5 Choose a frame from the Effects palette in Photoshop Elements.

Combining Photos and Text

Several years ago, some clever companies marketed stickers with various sayings that you could paste onto photo prints. Each saying was in a cartoon word bubble, and you could position them so it looked like the subjects in your photos were saying wacky things.

With an image editing program, you don't need stickers to add text to an image. Image editing programs offer a text tool for inserting text digitally. You can format the text to use any of the fonts available on your system, change the color of text, layer the text on top of a shape, and (in most programs) enhance the text with attributes such as a drop shadow.

Many image editing programs will add the text on a separate layer in the image, enabling you to move and reformat the text as needed. Likewise, any shapes you draw to use with the text will be placed on a separate layer. Although the process for adding text will vary from program to program, here's an example of how to add text and a shape behind the text to an image using Photoshop Elements:

1. Open the image to edit.
2. Choose the desired shape tool from the toolbox.
3. Choose desired settings for the shape, such as a fill color, on the Options bar above the image window.
4. Drag on the image to add the shape. The shape will appear on its own layer (see Figure 7.6).
5. Choose the Horizontal Type tool from the toolbox.
6. Choose desired settings for the text, such as font, size, and color, from the Options bar.
7. Click on the image and type the text. Once again, the text will appear on its own layer, as illustrated in Figure 7.7.
8. Click on the Commit (check mark) button at the right end of the Options bar to finish adding the text.

TIP

In most programs, the content you add for each new layer appears in front of or on top of the content you added previously. If your content doesn't appear in the correct order, you typically can correct that problem by changing the order of layers in the image. Consult the program's Help feature to learn about organizing content with layers.

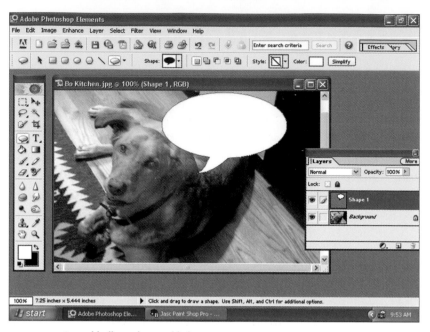

FIGURE 7.6 A word balloon shape added to an image.

FIGURE 7.7 Text added in front of the word balloon shape.

Converting to Black-and-White

Black-and-white images (called *grayscale images* in digital image editing programs) can have a journalistic or documentary feel. Grayscale images with high contrast look dramatic and can really highlight the subject in a picture. Even though you'll primarily be shooting pictures in color with your digital camera (unless your camera offers the ability to shoot in black-and-white or sepia and you often do so), you don't have to keep the color information in the image.

Whether you want to experiment with how a particular photo might look when converted to grayscale or you need to convert an image to grayscale for printing in a black-and-white publication, you can convert a color image to grayscale using your image editing program. In most image editing programs, the conversion is a simple matter of choosing a command such as Image, Greyscale (Paint Shop Pro) or Image, Mode, Grayscale (Photoshop Elements).

Figure 7.8 compares how an image looks before and after grayscale conversion. Adjusting brightness and contrast settings could make the grayscale version of the image even more dramatic.

7

FIGURE 7.8 The original image (left) and its grayscale counterpart (right).

FIGURE 7.9 A grayscale image with a single color added is called a duotone.

Trying an Image in Sepia

If you want alternative coloration for an image but grayscale seems too harsh, consider converting a color image to sepia tones. A sepia image looks somewhat like a grayscale image, but uses brown and off-white tones rather than shades of black and white. Sepia images look traditional and old-timey, as if they were from an old newspaper that has yellowed or were made with an old photo-developing technology, such as tin type. Photo processing labs have been able to print images in sepia tones for decades, and you can use your image editing software to try it yourself.

As with some of the other techniques presented in this chapter, the steps for converting an image to sepia differ greatly depending on which image editing software you use.

✦ Some programs offer a separate filter or command for converting an image to sepia. For example, in Paint Shop Pro, you can choose Effects, Artistic Effects, Sepia Toning, and then specify how far to age the image in the dialog box that appears (see Figure 7.10).

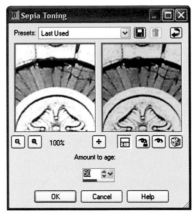

FIGURE 7.10 Adding a sepia effect to an image.

✦ In other programs, you have to use the colorize or color mixer feature to adjust the image so it has the brownish and creamy tones. In Photoshop Elements, for example, choose Enhance, Adjust Color, Hue/Saturation; click on the Colorize check box in the Hue/Saturation dialog box; and then click on OK.

Figure 7.11 compares an original color image to another copy of the image that has been converted to sepia tones.

FIGURE 7.11 The original image (left) and its sepia counterpart (right).

TIP

Convert an image to sepia and add a ragged or soft border to yield a romantic effect, which looks great for wedding photos.

Creating a Panorama or Collage

In Chapter 4, you learned that some cameras offer a panorama picture-taking mode that enables you to take pictures you can combine into a single panorama image using image editing software. Some programs, including some photo album programs, enable you to create a collage or scrapbook layout for a group of photos. Your camera's accessories also may have included software for creating panoramas.

You'll use steps like these from Photoshop Elements to combine images into a panorama or collage:

1. Open all of the images to combine.
2. Choose File, Create Photomerge.
3. Make sure the dialog box that appears (the Photomerge dialog box) lists all the photos to combine, and then click on OK.
4. If the program cannot align all the pictures as needed, it will display a message. Click on OK to close the message.
5. In the Photomerge dialog box, drag each of the pictures from the filmstrip above the image area to the image area.
6. Drag images to position them as desired in the picture (see Figure 7.12).
7. Click on OK to complete the merge.
8. Crop the new image file if required, and then save the file.

TIP

Even if your image editing program doesn't offer an automated command for creating a panorama or collage, you can do it manually. Create a large new image file with a blank or white background. Then, open each image you want to insert, resize it to a smaller size so it's much smaller than the size of the new image you created, select the entire image, and choose Edit, Copy to copy it. Close the image without saving the resizing change. Back in the new image, click on Edit, Paste to paste in the copied image. It will appear on its own layer so you can easily move and reposition it.

Drag each image from here...

...and position it here.

FIGURE 7.12 Drag the images to create a panorama or collage.

Managing Your Photo Library

In this chapter:

- ◆ Looking at your pictures in Windows XP
- ◆ Using Windows XP to copy or delete images
- ◆ Organizing your photos with album or catalog software
- ◆ Preserving or backing up your photos to CD-R

O nce you've started using your digital camera, it won't take long to accumulate hundreds of photos. Although a relatively new computer with a large hard disk drive can handle the volume, it's the electronic equivalent of a shoebox stuffed with pictures. You still have to apply your brain power to organize the photos in the way you prefer.

This chapter teaches you about basic techniques you can use to get a handle on all the images you've stuffed into your computer. You'll learn how to preview, copy, and delete images in Windows XP. Then, you will learn about software for managing photos as albums or catalogs. And finally, you'll see how to use Windows XP to create a CD-R of your images, as a backup or so that you can remove the images from your system to make room for others.

Previewing an Image in Windows XP

The XP upgrade of Microsoft's Windows operating system incorporated a number of new features for managing graphics, songs, and other types of media. For example, whenever you set up a new user under Windows XP, the system creates a My Pictures folder within the user's My Documents folder.

For easy access to the My Pictures folder, all you have to do is click on the Start button, and then click on My Pictures in the Start menu, as shown in Figure 8.1. The My Pictures folder typically uses one of two views—the Thumbnails view or the Filmstrip view. Both of these views help you work more effectively with the digital images you've transferred from your camera to your computer.

The Thumbnails view displays a large thumbnail image of each picture and folder. As you can see in Figure 8.2, if a folder holds pictures, then the folder thumbnail previews some of the pictures in the folder.

The Filmstrip view also shows a large thumbnail of each folder and image, but it arranges them along the bottom of the window in a scrolling strip. Use the scroll arrow along the bottom of the window to scroll the strip to the left or right. When you click on a picture in the strip, a larger preview of the picture will appear in the preview portion of the window, as shown in Figure 8.3.

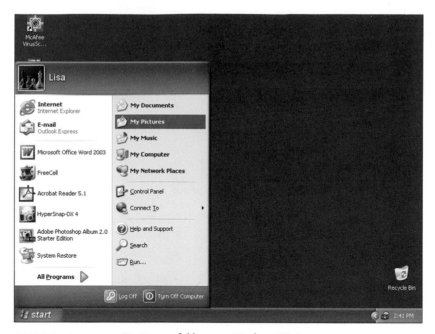

FIGURE 8.1 Access your My Pictures folder using Windows XP's Start menu.

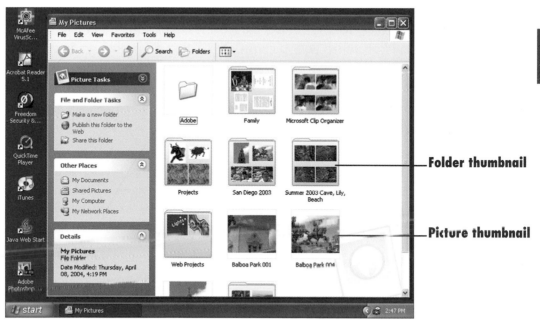

Folder thumbnail

Picture thumbnail

FIGURE 8.2 Browse through your pictures more effectively in the Thumbnails view.

Preview of selected picture

Filmstrip

FIGURE 8.3 Use the Filmstrip view to view an even larger picture preview.

Windows XP actually enables you to apply the Thumbnails or Filmstrip view when you're viewing files in any folder, not just the My Pictures folder. You have the flexibility you need to store and organize your pictures anywhere you prefer, while still taking advantage of XP's features for working with images. In addition, you can use the Filmstrip view to rotate images that you've shot in a tall (portrait) orientation, rather than the wide orientation of most pictures. Follow these steps to work with a folder of pictures in Filmstrip view:

1. Open a folder window on the Windows XP desktop and navigate to the folder that holds the pictures.
2. Click on the View menu, and then click on Filmstrip. The window will display the Filmstrip view.
3. To see the large preview of an image, drag the scroll bar and then click on the desired image in the filmstrip. Or, click on the Previous Image and Next Image buttons (see Figure 8.4) to view the photos one by one.
4. To rotate an image to the proper orientation, click on the Rotate Clockwise or Rotate Counterclockwise button.

NOTE

Windows XP automatically resaves the image with the new rotation applied so you don't have to rotate it again in the future.

---

5. To see information about an image, such as the date it was taken, point to the image thumbnail in the filmstrip. A yellow tip with image information will pop up.

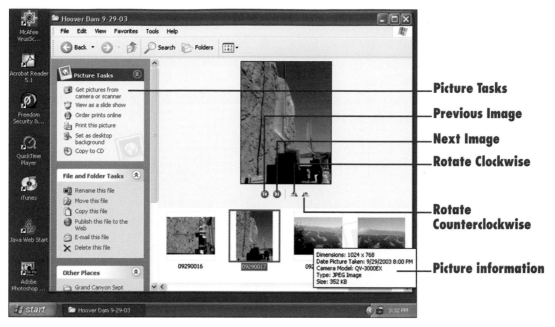

Picture Tasks

Previous Image

Next Image

Rotate Clockwise

Rotate Counterclockwise

Picture information

FIGURE 8.4 Navigating in the Filmstrip view.

6 Finally, when you open a folder that holds pictures in Windows XP, the list of tasks at the left side of the folder window will change to include a Picture Tasks category. Click on the double-arrow button to the right of the category name to open the category, and then choose the action you want to perform on the selected picture or on the files in the folder.

8

TIP

Windows XP can display all the pictures in your My Pictures folder (and its subfolders) as your screensaver. Right-click on the desktop, and then click on Properties. Click on the Screen Saver tab in the Display Properties dialog box. Open the Screen Saver drop-down list and click on My Pictures Slideshow. Specify the Wait interval (how long your computer must be idle before the screensaver starts), and then click on OK.

Copying and Deleting Images in Windows XP

As with other types of files, you might want to copy your image files to another location or delete them when you no longer need them. The list of tasks in the Windows XP window makes it easy to complete any copy or move operation.

Use these steps to copy or delete image files in a Windows XP folder window:

1. In any view, select the file(s) to copy. You can hold down the Shift key while you click to select multiple adjacent files, or you can hold down the Ctrl key while you click to select multiple nonadjacent files. (In the Filmstrip view, select the thumbnails in the filmstrip.)
2. Click on the Copy the Selected Items link in the File and Folder Tasks section of the list of tasks at the left side of the window. The Copy Items dialog box will open.

> **TIP**
>
> You can click on the Move the Selected Items link to move the image files. Also, Windows XP still enables you to use the Cut, Copy, and Paste commands on the Edit menu to copy or move files between open folder windows.

3. In the Copy Items dialog box (see Figure 8.5), select the disk and folder to which you want to copy the files.
4. Click on Copy. Windows XP will copy the files.
5. When you're ready to delete one or more files, select them in any view.
6. Click on the Delete the Selected Items link in the File and Folder Tasks section of the list of tasks at the left side of the window, or press the Delete key. A dialog box will prompt you to confirm the deletion, as shown in Figure 8.6.

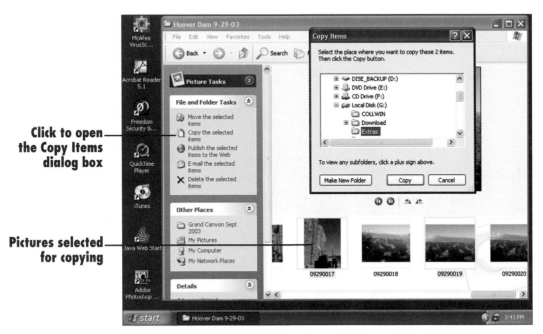

FIGURE 8.5 Copy image files to another folder just as you would any other file.

FIGURE 8.6 Windows XP prompts you to confirm any file deletion.

7 Click on Yes to send the image files to the Recycle Bin on the desktop.

8 To delete the images permanently, right-click on the Recycle Bin icon at any time, and then click on Empty Recycle Bin. Click on Yes in the confirmation dialog box that appears to finish the permanent deletion.

Looking at Photo Album Software for Managing Images

Earlier I compared the collection of photos on your computer to a shoebox full of photos. Given the number of photos you've accumulated by now, it's probably more like a library. Even though Windows XP offers some great features for managing your images, you might wish you had your own personal librarian to help manage the digital images on your computer. That's where photo album software comes in.

> **Photo album software** imports all your pictures into a digital library and manages your pictures from that central location. You can organize images from the library into separate albums or collections, print images, order prints, and more.

Using photo album software, you can import all your images from various disks and folders, directly from your camera, or from a CD-R or Kodak Picture CD into a centralized library. (The program might make copies of the imported files, or it might simply reference them in their original location on the disk.) From there, you can do a variety of things with the images, depending on the capabilities of the photo album software you select.

✦ **Organize photos into albums.** You can use any criteria you want to group photos into an album, such as including the best photos from a particular vacation (see Figure 8.7). Once you've placed the images together in an album, you can perform operations that apply to the entire group of photos, such as burning the entire group to a CD-R.

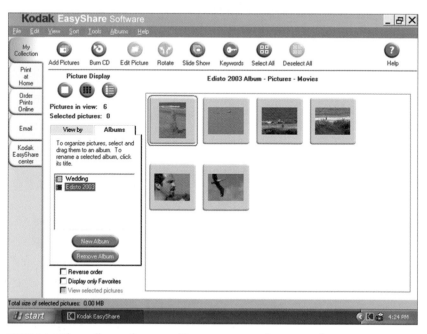

FIGURE 8.7 Photo album software enables you to group photos into albums.

✦ **Assign keywords, tags, or titles to photos.** Storing additional information to identify your photos makes finding and sorting photos easier.

✦ **Edit individual photos.** Basic photo album programs offer tools for rotating and cropping pictures. Other album programs, such as Adobe Photoshop Album 2.0 Starter Edition, shown in Figure 8.8, provide even more powerful tools for correcting color, removing red-eye, or adding attractive frames to photos.

✦ **Print photos.** All photo album programs enable you to print one or more selected photos, either as plain printouts or in standard photo sizes, such as 4×6, 5×7, and so on. Most also will print multiple selected images as a *contact sheet* or *picture package*.

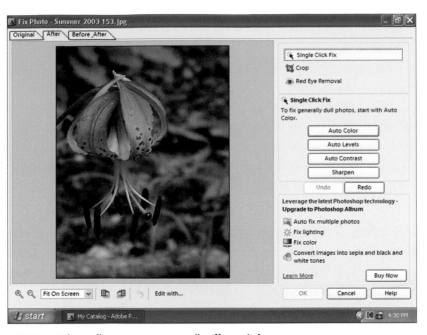

FIGURE 8.8 Photo album programs typically offer tools for correcting your images.

A **contact sheet** is a printout of multiple photos on a single page that presents each photo as a small thumbnail. This enables you to show a large number of photos to someone else for the purpose of selecting the best photos. A **picture package**, in contrast, repeats a single image in multiple sizes on a single page to use paper efficiently.

8

+ **Order photos online.** Most photo album programs enable you to connect with one or more online photo processing services to have high-quality prints made of your images. By default, the Adobe Photoshop Album 2.0 Starter Edition enables you to order prints from PhotoAccess Print Processing and Shutterfly. Chapter 11, "Transforming Photos into Keepsakes," offers more information about ordering prints online.

+ **Share pictures electronically.** Even basic photo album programs enable you to send photos as e-mail attachments, and most let you display the images in an album as a slideshow. The best also enable you to set up a photo album online as a Web page so others can log on and view your photos at their convenience.

Although the scope of this book doesn't allow me to show you how to perform every operation in each photo album program, the preceding list should give you an idea of what's possible. There are a number of good album programs out there, so you might want to consider several before you choose one. Here's a list of possibilities:

✦ While Windows XP doesn't include photo album software per se, it does let you accomplish a few actions with regard to photos when you're working in a folder that contains pictures. When you navigate to a folder that contains pictures, the Picture Tasks list appears at the left. You can click the View as a Slideshow link to play a slideshow of all the pictures in the current folder. Or, click the Order Prints Online link to start the Online Print Ordering Wizard. As shown in Figure 8.9, this wizard enables you to select one or more images in the folder to have prints made by one of a number of partner print services.

✦ If you're a Mac user, you need iPhoto 4 (http://www.apple.com/iphoto). In addition to the regular features, this program offers Rendezvous photo sharing over a network, photo ratings, professional-quality slideshow transitions, the ability to use iTunes music with slideshows, the ability to have bound photo books printed, and a Smart Album feature that finds photos based on criteria you specify and builds the album for you.

✦ Your camera's software CD might include a proprietary album program, such as the Kodak EasyShare program shown in Figure 8.7. This well-rounded album program comes with Kodak cameras and includes many of the same features as

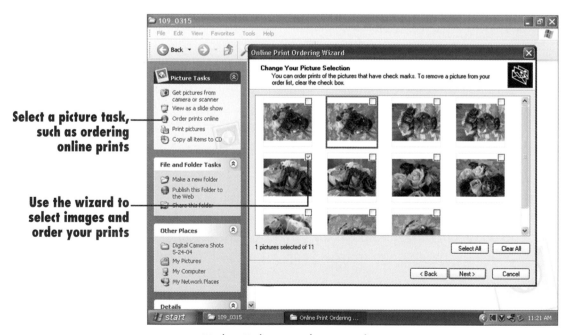

Select a picture task, such as ordering online prints

Use the wizard to select images and order your prints

FIGURE 8.9 Windows XP lets you order prints online.

album programs sold by major software companies. Install the software that comes with your camera and check it out to see whether it includes an album program.

♦ Consider the leader, Adobe Photoshop Album 2.0. This program always gets good reviews from users of all skill levels. For more information about the software, see Adobe (http://www.adobe.com/products/photoshopalbum). Or, you can download the free version, Adobe Photoshop Album 2.0 Starter Edition (refer to Figure 8.8) from http://www.adobe.com/products/photoshopalbum/ starter.html. Even the Starter Edition gives you the ability to correct a variety of image tone and quality problems, order prints online, create slideshows, and share pictures via e-mail or the Web. The retail version adds cool features like the ability to create printed albums (such as scrapbooks), greeting cards, electronic greeting cards, calendars, photo books, and more.

♦ Paint Shop Photo Album is from a software company called Jasc Software, Inc. (http://www.jasc.com). You can download a free trial version of the software from the Jasc Web site. In addition to handling the usual photo album tasks, this software enables you to add a decorative picture frame, create panoramas, make slideshows with captions and sound, use its Thinify tool to make photo subjects look thinner, use templates to create attractive scrapbook page layouts, and more.

♦ If you didn't receive an album program with your camera and you don't want to pay full retail prices, you can check out shareware sites, such as Download.com (http://www.download.com), to see what smaller software authors are offering. A number of lesser-known album programs are available, and most shareware sites provide reviews and user ratings to help you select a program to try and buy. If you continue using the shareware program, remember to send the requested shareware fee to the company or individual who created the software.

TIP

Some online photo services also offer free software that you can use to manage your images. One example, is Snapfish (http://www.snapfish.com). For more on online photo services, see Chapter 11, "Transforming Photos into Keepsakes."

Burning Your Photos to a CD-R in Windows XP

Another way to organize photos is to burn a collection of related photos to a single CD-R (or a rewritable CD-RW). You can do this to create a backup of your photo files so your photos aren't lost if something happens to your computer or hard disk. Or, you can transfer images to CD-R to make room on your hard drive for more current photos.

CAUTION

Although CD-Rs provide a relatively stable and durable backup medium, they are not indestructible. You should store them in some type of jewel case or sleeve to prevent scratches. Some people maintain that sunlight can damage the polycarbonate and other materials used to make CD-Rs so they should be stored out of direct sunlight. Finally, extreme heat can warp, so store them in a location with relatively low and stable temperatures. Even better, the next time you buy a new computer or drive, go for a DVD-R drive. Not only do DVD-Rs hold more content, but your backups will remain usable longer should CD technology be phased out in favor of DVD.

Even if you don't purchase photo album software that gives you an automated way to burn an album of photos to a CD-R, you can still get the job done with Windows XP. Windows XP includes built-in CD-R–burning capabilities you can use if your system has a CD-R drive (or CD burner drive) installed—that is, a drive that can write or burn CD-Rs, unlike a CD-ROM drive, which can only read CD media.

NOTE

Ideally, you want to save backup copies of the highest resolution (largest) version of each image file. That way, you can always resize the backup image to a smaller size when needed. The image file sizes will determine how many images you can burn to each CD-R. With CD-R media becoming cheaper by the day, the main investment in saving the larger files will be using more of your time to burn more CD-Rs.

Follow these steps to burn your photos to CD-R in Windows XP:

1. Insert a blank CD-R into the CD-R drive. Windows will display a dialog box that asks you what you want to do.
2. Leave Open Writable CD Folder using Windows Explorer selected and click on OK (see Figure 8.10). A folder window for the CD-R will open.
3. Click on the window's Minimize button to minimize the window to a taskbar button.

FIGURE 8.10 After you insert a CD-R, leave
the first option selected and then click on OK.

④ Open your My Pictures folder or any other folder that holds the pictures you want to burn to CD-R.

⑤ In any view, select the file(s) or folder(s) to copy to the CD-R folder. You can hold down the Shift key while you click to select multiple adjacent files, or you can hold down the Ctrl key while you click to select multiple nonadjacent files.

⑥ In the list of tasks at the left side of the window, click on the double-arrow button beside the Picture Tasks category to expand the category (see Figure 8.11).

Click to copy your selection to the CD-R folder

Folders selected for burning

FIGURE 8.11 After you select the items to burn to CD-R, use the Copy to CD task to copy them to the CD-R folder.

Burning Your Photos to a CD-R in Windows XP 125

7 Click on the Copy to CD task. Windows XP will create temporary copies of the selected file(s) and folder(s) in the CD-R folder.

NOTE

If the Picture Tasks category doesn't appear in the task list (most likely because the folder you're working with contains only other folders and no individual image files), you can select a folder to copy and choose File, Send To, CD Drive (*CD-R drive letter:*) to place copies of the images in the CD-R drive folder for burning.

---

8 Repeat Steps 4 through 7 as needed to continue identifying pictures and folders to be burned to the CD-R.

9 When you've finished selecting files and folders, click on the CD-R folder's taskbar button. The folder window will reopen.

10 In the CD Writing Tasks category in the task list at the left, click on the Write These Files to CD task (see Figure 8.12). The Windows XP CD Writing Wizard will open.

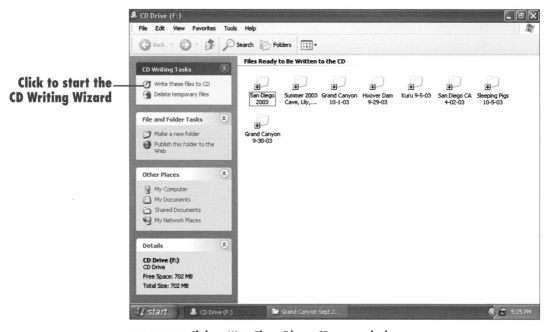

Click to start the CD Writing Wizard

FIGURE 8.12 Click on Write These Files to CD to start the burn.

⑪ Type a volume name to use for the CD in the CD Name text box, and then click on Next (see Figure 8.13). The CD Writing Wizard will inform you of its progress as it writes the data to the CD-R. When it finishes, the wizard ejects the CD and displays its final screen.

FIGURE 8.13 Enter a CD-R name when you are prompted by the CD Writing Wizard.

TIP

Naming each CD-R is a good practice so the Windows XP My Computer window can display the CD-R's name when you insert the disc.

⑫ Click on Finish. The wizard window will close.
⑬ Use a permanent marker to label the CD as needed, and store it in a safe place.

PART III

Sharing Your Photos with the World

Printing Your Photos

In this chapter:

- ✦ Choosing inkjet printer settings
- ✦ Printing to special photo paper or greeting card stock
- ✦ Printing a contact sheet of photos
- ✦ Printing from a cradle printer
- ✦ Printing right from the camera or storage medium
- ✦ Getting prints from a retailer

Although an image on a computer screen might look great, you can't take it with you in your wallet to show off to friends and family. According to a recent study commissioned by Fujifilm USA that was performed by InfoTrends Research Group, Inc., about 92 percent of digital camera users say they make their own photo prints at home.

This chapter will explore various methods of photo printing. You'll learn how to work with inkjet printer settings to complete various print jobs—from a basic print to something more snazzy, such as a photo greeting card. You will see how to use a cradle printer or a printer that enables you to connect a camera or insert camera storage media. Finally, you'll learn more about printing from a retail kiosk.

A Word about Inkjet Printers

Today's inkjet printers are a steal. You can purchase a printer that makes terrific 4×6 prints (and perhaps some larger sizes) for $150 or less. Invest a bit more, and you'll get a printer that prints at a higher print resolution and can produce larger images. If you haven't yet purchased a printer to make your photo prints, factor these points into your decision process:

◆ **Print resolution.** Print resolution provides an indication of the quality of output a printer can produce, just as a camera's resolution gives an indication of the quality of output the camera can produce. Printer resolutions are stated in *dpi*, with larger values being better. A larger number of dots per inch means that each dot must be smaller, yielding a finer image. Resolutions can be stated in two dimensions (as in 4800×1200) or one (as in max. resolution 5760). For the best photo quality and greatest flexibility in printout size, choose the printer with the highest resolution capability possible. When comparing printers, also look at the size of the ink drops in picoliters. The smaller the ink drops, the finer the print.

Print resolution refers to the fineness of a printout, measured in dpi (*dots per inch*).

◆ **Print speed.** There's usually a tradeoff between print speed and print quality (but not always), so decide which is most important to you and choose your printer accordingly. Read reviews of printer hardware online (http://www.pcmag.com/reviews or http://reviews.cnet.com).

◆ **Number of ink colors and maintenance.** Some top inkjet printers now offer six, seven, or eight ink colors. Although more ink colors enable a printer to produce more lifelike colors, they also might mean you need to keep more different ink cartridges on hand to be sure you have a replacement when one of the cartridges runs out.

◆ **Borderless prints and photos sizes.** If you want to make prints without a white border (that is, prints that bleed off the edges of the paper), choose a printer with borderless print capabilities. Also, be aware that some less expensive inkjet printers and some specialized printers, such as cradle printers, can only print 4×6 prints and no larger sizes. If you want larger prints, look for a printer that can handle paper sizes larger than 4×6.

9

FIGURE 9.1 A Dell photo printer.

◆ **Interface type.** Virtually all inkjet printers connect via USB, but many use the older USB 1.1 standard. If your computer offers a faster USB 2.0 port or a FireWire port, look for a printer with the same type of interface. When the computer can transfer images to the printer more quickly over a speedier connection, you'll get your prints faster. Some printers also offer adapters for printing directly from Bluetooth-equipped and infrared (IrDA) wireless devices, such as digital cameras and camcorders, PDAs, and mobile phones with picture-taking capabilities.

CAUTION

Some printers don't include the USB or FireWire cable needed to connect to the computer; others might not include the ink cartridges. Be sure to check the printer packaging or online details about what's included with the printer to make sure you pick up any accessories you need.

◆ **Printer type.** Although they are increasing, compact inkjet printers can still hog quite a bit of desk space. If space is at a premium, consider a photo dock printer or one of the smaller units dedicated to making 4×6 prints.

◆ **Direct print from camera or storage media.** Some inkjet printers enable you to skip the hassle of booting up your PC and transferring images. If this sounds appealing to you, look for a printer with a USB interface for printing directly from your camera. Or, look for a printer that lets you insert storage media, such as CompactFlash, Memory Stick, Secure Digital, SmartMedia, or xD Picture Card cards.

◆ **Operating systems supported.** Some newer printers do not work with older operating systems, such as Windows versions prior to Windows 2000 and XP, or Mac OS versions prior to Mac OS X. Make sure that any printer you're considering will work with your operating system, or consider upgrading to a new computer system, too, for maximum speed and compatibility.

Making a Basic Print and Choosing Inkjet Printer Settings

As with any other piece of hardware, you need to set up your inkjet printer and install its software to enable it to work with Windows or the Mac OS. (Consult the instructions that shipped with your printer to learn how to set it up.) From there, the fun begins and you can start creating brilliant prints from your images.

TIP

Your photos will look better when they are printed on one of the fine specialty inkjet papers available today. Printer manufacturers such as Epson and Dell offer their own lines of photo papers, including precut paper for 4×6 prints or greeting cards, for example. Papers might have matte, glossy, or special linen appearances. The large office-supply chains also offer their own brands of photo and inkjet papers.

The exact steps for printing will vary slightly depending on whether you're printing from an image editing application, such as Photoshop Elements or Paint Shop Pro, or a photo album application, such as Adobe Photoshop Album or Paint Shop Photo Album. Here's an overview of how to start the process, choose print-quality settings for your printer, and send a regular printout to the printer:

1. Power up the printer and insert the desired type of paper as directed by the printer's user manual.
2. Start the application from which you want to print.
3. If you're working in an image editing program, open the image you want to print, and then choose File, Print.
   OR
   If you're working in an album program, open the album holding the photo(s) to print, and then select the photo(s). Then, choose File, Print or the print command for the application you're using (see Figure 9.2).

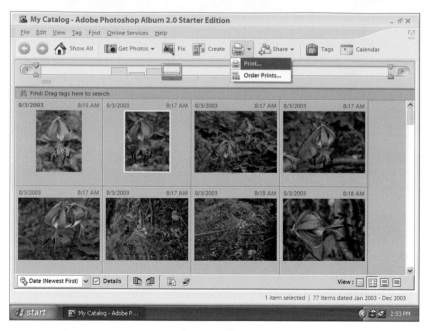

FIGURE 9.2 Starting to print an image from an album program.

④ In the Print window or dialog box that appears, choose the printer to which you want to print from the Name or Select Printer drop-down list. The printer will appear.

⑤ Click on the Properties or Preferences button to open the Properties dialog box for your printer (see Figure 9.3). The available properties and the dialog box appearance will vary depending on the printer's capabilities and the nature of the printer software.

⑥ Choose the desired settings. For example, choose the paper type and size and the quality setting. Figure 9.4 illustrates the Properties dialog box for my printer.

TIP

Typically, the quality setting determines the amount of ink applied to the printout (along with the selected paper type). More ink generally results in a brighter, better-quality image. If you're printing a document with only black-and-white text, choosing the Text or Black and White option will speed the print job and make sure the document is rendered using fewer inks.

---

⑦ Click on OK. The specified print settings will be applied.

⑧ Back in the Print dialog box or window, choose the appropriate settings, such as the print size (which should match the paper) and the layout.

⑨ Click on Print to send the image(s) to the printer.

⑩ Let the image dry, if necessary. When you're printing on certain types of paper, such as glossy photo paper, touching the image too soon will smudge it.

136 Printing Your Photos

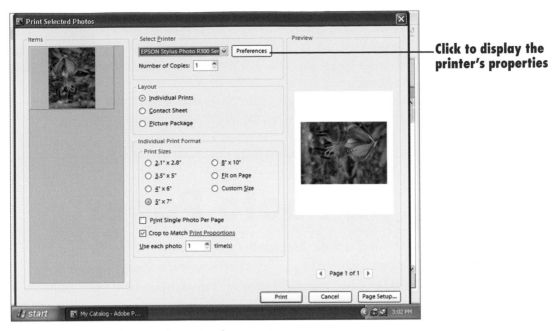

Click to display the printer's properties

FIGURE 9.3 Starting to choose quality settings for your printer.

FIGURE 9.4 The Properties dialog box enables you to control print-quality settings for your inkjet or photo printer.

9

Printing on Photo Paper

Photo prints you purchase from a retailer for standard 4×6 prints are pricey, plus you have to wait to get them. When you make your own prints, you not only save money, but you also get instant gratification. You can frame and display or send your prints to a loved one right away. And, if you have photo editing software, you can experiment with different effects and print your creations right away.

Most inkjet and photo printer manufacturers offer photo paper specially optimized for their printers and inks. The papers come in a variety of finishes, weights, and sizes, but they generally represent a good value when stacked up against the cost of retail prints, even when you factor in sales tax and a small expense for the ink used.

The process for printing on photo paper works as described earlier, with a few additional considerations:

◆ You have to make sure the image has a high enough resolution for the print size you want. Otherwise, even a great printer might not produce a good photo print.

◆ You have to make sure you insert the photo paper correctly, as instructed by the printer's user manual. Whether you insert the paper face up or face down is crucial, and it might depend on which paper tray you use for a given printer. When you're using small paper sizes, the printer might require you to insert the paper in the portrait (tall) orientation, even when you are printing the image in landscape (wide) orientation. And 4×6 papers typically have a perforated end that you tear off after the print dries; generally the end opposite the perforated end is the one to insert into the printer. Some printers also can print from rolls of photo paper rather than precut sheets.

◆ You have to make sure you open the Properties dialog box for the printer (see Figure 9.5) as described in the preceding section and choose the paper size and type that matches the paper size and type you've inserted. Otherwise, the printer might not use enough ink or position the image correctly on the paper, or it might not be able to feed the paper correctly.

FIGURE 9.5 Display the printer properties and choose the paper type and size that matches the photo paper you've inserted. For example, the settings here are for 4×6 glossy prints.

◆ If required by your printer, you might need to choose File, Page Setup, and then choose Sheet (Borderless) from the Source dialog box to make the prints borderless. Some printers can make borderless prints without special page setup choices.

TIP

Some inkjet printers will even print on sticker stock, printable CD-Rs, iron-on paper, and more. If you're considering a particular printer model and you might be interested in printing more than just prints, go online to the manufacturer's Web site, see which media the printer can print on, and check the manufacturer's prices for the actual paper or media.

Printing on Greeting Card Stock

Printing your own greeting cards can be trickier—a lot trickier, especially if you're choosing to use a paper that's not from the same manufacturer as your printer. Overall, the process is the same. You insert the paper as specified by your printer, choose the appropriate paper size and type settings from the Properties dialog box for the printer, choose settings for the print job in the Print dialog box or window, and then click on Print. Although that might sound easy, you might actually burn through a few bad printouts before you get it right. Here are a few tips for doing that:

◆ Check with the software you're using to see whether it includes templates or other settings for generating greeting card printouts. For example, Figure 9.6 shows a Paint Shop Pro template being used to print four postcards.

◆ If your card stock comes on larger perforated sheets, you might get better results by separating the cards and then printing to them. For example, if you've purchased panel cards (postcards) that are four to a sheet, perforating them and creating a custom paper size might help. To create a custom paper size, open the Properties dialog box for your printer from the Print dialog box or window. Go to the tab or the drop-down list for choosing paper size, and then click on the Custom or User-Defined choice. Enter the desired paper dimensions and a name for the custom paper, as shown in Figure 9.7, and then click on Save or OK. Or, depending on the printer you're using, you might have the option to scale the printout to a particular percentage to help it fit on the card stock.

◆ If you're printing on a folding card, remember that the image has to print on only half of the front side. This means you'll have to set up the printout manually if the printer you're using doesn't accommodate the paper style you've selected. In photo editing software, this would involve creating a new blank image file that's the same size as the greeting card paper, and then positioning the actual

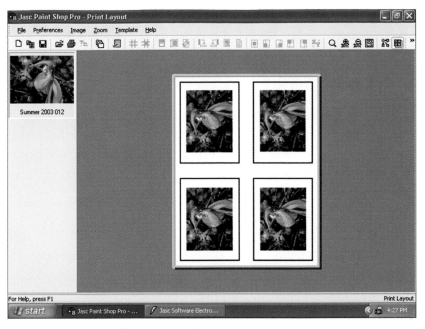

FIGURE 9.6 Using a template to print cards.

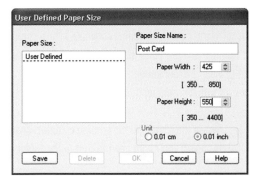

FIGURE 9.7 You can create a custom paper size to fit your greeting card stock.

image file on either the bottom (for top-fold cards) or the right (for left-fold cards) half of the larger image.

✦ If you're printing on matte paper, remember that you might be able to turn each printed card over and print a greeting on the other side. If that's what you want to do, consider printing the greeting side first because it has less ink that can smear. After you print that side and allow it to dry, print the photo side.

Printing a Contact Sheet or Picture Package

As noted in Chapter 8, a contact sheet includes a thumbnail of each image in a group of images (typically images stored in the same folder on your hard disk, images in the same album, or images you've selected from a library), while a picture package prints multiple copies of a single image at varying sizes on a single page.

> **TIP**
>
> A picture package gives you an economical way to make prints on larger, less expensive (relatively speaking) 8.5×11 photo paper. It's worth investing in an inexpensive paper trimmer, available at office supply stores for $15 or so, to make clean cuts when you separate the images.

To print a contact sheet or picture package:

1. If required in your software, select the album or images to include in the contact sheet or picture package. (This is typically the case with album software, not image editing software.) For a contact sheet (see Figure 9.8), you need to select the entire album or multiple images. For a picture package (see Figure 9.9), select one or more images to print a picture package sheet of each selected image.

2. In your photo album software, choose the command to start a print job.
   OR
   In your image editing program, choose the command for printing a contact sheet or picture package, such as File, Print Layout, Contact Sheet. (At this point, you might need to choose the folder holding the images to include in the contact sheet.)

3. Choose overall print settings, such as the page size. You might need to go to the printer's Properties dialog box to do so, or you might simply work in the dialog box or window for creating the picture package or contact sheet.

4. Choose layout settings for the contact sheet or picture package (refer to Figures 9.8 and 9.9). For a contact sheet, you might be able to specify the number of columns per sheet. For a picture package, you can choose the size and number of prints included in the package.

5. Finish all other print settings. For example, you might be able to use the Page Setup command to make further page size and layout changes.

6. Send the job to the printer.

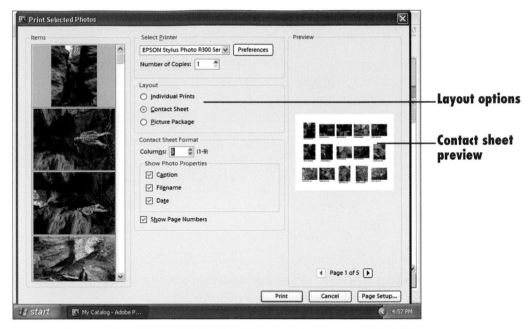

Layout options

Contact sheet preview

FIGURE 9.8 A contact sheets shows all of the selected images or those in a particular folder or album.

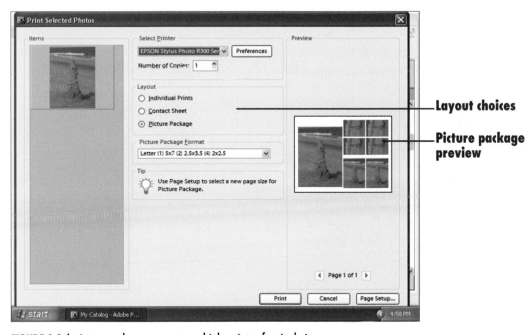

Layout choices

Picture package preview

9

FIGURE 9.9 A picture package presents multiple prints of a single image per page.

Printing via a Cradle Printer

Some devices you can buy to accompany your digital camera serve a dual role as a dock or cradle *and* a photo printer. When connected to your computer, these devices provide a convenient way to transfer and print pictures.

Even better, most photo docks can print even when they're not connected to a computer. You can literally walk into the room, turn the cradle or dock printer on, seat the camera in the holder (as shown in Figure 9.10), and press a Print button to make prints. As you can see from Figure 9.10, you trade some flexibility for convenience. Cradle or dock printers generally can only print 4×6 images, like most dedicated photo printing devices.

If you decide to go the cradle or dock printer route, of course you'll have to buy the one that's compatible with your camera, offered by your camera's manufacturer. After you

FIGURE 9.10 A cradle or dock printer can make prints from the camera even when the cradle or dock is not connected to a computer.

purchase the dock, set it up per the device's user manual. This will involve inserting some type of printing film and a loaded paper tray, and perhaps snapping in a custom insert that will help your camera seat correctly. If you want to use the dock to transfer images to the computer, connect it to the computer via a USB cable (which you might have to purchase separately), and then run the installation software as indicated in the user manual.

Here's how to use your camera and dock together to make 4×6 prints:

1. With the camera powered on, use its preview or review feature to look through the images stored on its internal storage card. When you see an image you want to print, press the button or choose the appropriate menu command for sharing and printing the image. For example, for a Kodak EasyShare camera, you would press the Share button on the back of the camera, use an arrow key on the rocker/controller button to select the print icon in the LCD display, and then press the OK button. Continue marking images for printing in this manner as needed.

2. Power down the camera and put on its lens cap.

3. Open the sliding door that protects the camera dock connector, as shown in Figure 9.11.

4. Seat the camera in the dock.

5. Press the dock's power button to turn it on.

6. Press the dock's print button. The dock will read the photo data from the camera and print the specified image(s).

CAUTION

Of course, choosing a cradle or dock printer or any dedicated photo printer locks you into using a particular brand of photo paper. Before you purchase a dock printer or dedicated photo printer, check to see what paper types it can use to ensure you'll be able to make the types of prints you want and that you won't have trouble finding more photo paper when you need to replenish your supply.

9

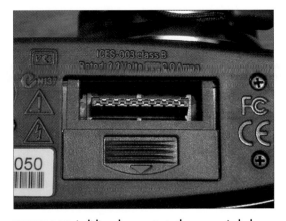

FIGURE 9.11 A sliding door protects the camera's dock connector. Open this door before docking the camera in the cradle or dock printer.

Printing Directly from a Camera or Storage Media

Some full-featured inkjet printers also offer you an alternative if you want to print directly from a camera or storage medium without first transferring the images to a computer.

A number of great printers on the market enable you to print directly from a camera connected to the computer, as long as the camera supports an image transfer protocol (such as DPOF or PictBridge) compatible with the printer's requirements. Some printers might also enable you to insert a storage card with images from your camera and print directly from the storage card. For example, many photo printer models can print from inserted CompactFlash, IBM Microdrive, Memory Stick, Secure Digital, MMC (MultiMediaCard), SmartMedia, or xD Picture Card media types.

> **CAUTION**
>
> Check the printer's user manual to see what its limits are in printing from a particular medium. For example, the printer might only be able to handle certain image types, such as JPEG and TIFF, and it might only be able to read a limited number of images from the medium, such as a maximum of 999.

The process for printing from a compatible camera or inserted storage medium is roughly the same as a regular print job, once you make the proper connections:

1. Power up the printer and insert the desired type of paper.
2. With the camera powered off, connect it via its USB cable to the USB port for the camera (see Figure 9.12), typically found on the front of the printer. Then power the camera on or place it in its playback or preview mode. The printer will read the images stored in the camera.
   OR
   Remove the storage card from the camera and insert it into the appropriate slot on the printer (refer to Figure 9.12). The printer will read the images stored on the card.
3. Use the printer's menu settings (see Figure 9.13) to choose which image to print and make your choices for other available settings, such as number of copies, paper size, and layout. Generally, you'll use arrow buttons on the printer to highlight a menu item, and then press the OK or select button to select the highlighted item.

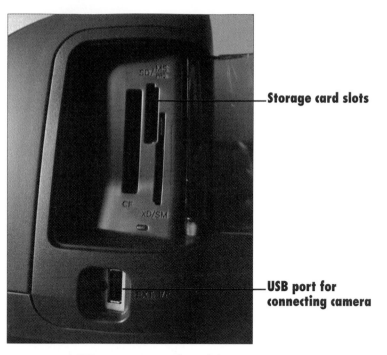

Storage card slots

USB port for
connecting camera

FIGURE 9.12 A USB connection or media card slot enables the printer to print directly from a camera or storage card.

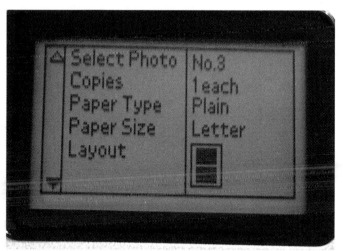

Select Photo   No.3
Copies   1 each
Paper Type   Plain
Paper Size   Letter
Layout

FIGURE 9.13 The printer menu enables you to choose which image and how many copies to print.

④ Press the print button on the printer. The printer will read the camera storage or inserted storage card, identify the selected image(s), and print.

⑤ When the print job finishes and the print light stops flashing, disconnect the camera and power it off. Or, remove the storage card by pressing the Eject button (if any) and pulling the card straight out. Do not remove the storage card if the card reader indicator light is blinking; otherwise, you'll damage the card contents.

Printing at a Retailer

Last but not least, retailers in your area might bridge the gap for you if your inkjet printer conks out or if you don't want to spring for a photo-quality printer at home. Many major retail chains—such as Wal-Mart, Kmart, CVS, and other major drugstores, supermarkets, and other general merchandise retailers—have in-store kiosks that enable you to print images from your digital storage media, including images burned to CD-R, Kodak Picture CD, and floppy disk. Prices start at 24 cents per 4×6 print. You get to choose which images you want from the storage medium, and in some cases you can make corrections to the photos or crop them. Once you order the prints, you can shop for a few minutes, and they will be processed before you leave the store.

Here's how to use a retail kiosk to get prints from your digital photo storage medium:

① Identify the storage medium that has the image(s) to print and take it to your local retailer that offers a print kiosk.

② Insert the storage medium into the appropriate slot as directed on the kiosk.

③ Use the kiosk touch screen to select the image(s) to print and make corrections such as cropping, if the option is available.

④ Choose the print command, provide payment information as prompted, and specify details such as how many prints to make and whether to also burn the images to a Kodak Picture CD.

⑤ Shop for a while, and then return to retrieve your prints.

10

Sharing Photos Digitally

In this chapter:

+ Sharing your digital photos via e-mail
+ Adding a photo to a Web page you've designed
+ Creating a photo gallery to share online
+ Creating and sharing a photo slideshow
+ Sharing images from your picture phone

Most people still participate in a time-honored tradition: sharing pictures of the latest trip/soccer game/school play/milestone/and so on with loved ones around the country and the world. That process used to involve ordering extra sets of photo prints, waiting for the prints to be completed, popping the finished prints in the mail (with the obligatory greeting and explanatory note), and then promising anxious recipients that the pictures were on the way.

Today, there's no waiting around. As soon as you snap a shot from your digital camera and transfer it to your computer, you can share it with friends and family all over the world. This chapter will show you how to share or publish your photos instantly using a variety of methods. You'll learn how to e-mail photos and include them in Web pages. You will see how to set up your own online photo gallery, using either your own Web space or space from an online photo service. After seeing how to create your own slideshow from selected pictures, you'll learn more about sharing images that you've shot with a picture phone.

E-Mailing a Photo

I'll take e-mail over snail mail (mail delivered on the ground by the agency of your choice) any day. While e-mail isn't instant, e-mail usually is able to make it across the Internet in hours or less. I've even had nieces living in Egypt e-mail photos that arrived minutes after they were sent.

If you've just snapped the photo of a lifetime, this section shows you how to shoot it to friends and relatives using the most direct and personal method: e-mail. You can choose one of two methods for sending a digital picture via e-mail: attaching it to an e-mail message using your e-mail program or sending it from within your photo editing or album software.

From an E-Mail Program

You don't need any special image software to send a digital image file via e-mail. All you need is your e-mail program. While the example here shows e-mail from the Outlook® Express program that comes with Windows XP, virtually all e-mail programs enable you to follow a similar process to send a photo as a file attachment to a message.

CAUTION

Because picture files are large and most e-mail providers limit the size of the files that you can attach to an e-mail message (between 2M and 10M, typically), you'll have to limit the number of pictures you attach to any particular e-mail program. Otherwise, you can compress several pictures into one smaller file using the Compressed (zipped) Folder feature in Windows XP or separate compression software such as WinZip (http://www.winzip.com). Of course, if the e-mail recipient has a slow dial-up connection, you'll want to limit the size of attached files to less than 1M.

Follow these steps to e-mail a digital photo as a file attachment:

1. Start the e-mail program.
2. Click the Create Mail button, or use the button or command for creating a new e-mail message in your software.
3. Enter the recipient's e-mail address in the To: text box.
4. Enter the message subject in the Subject: text box.
5. Type the message contents in the message body area of the message window.
6. Click on the Attach button; choose Insert, File Attachment or choose the command for attaching a file to a message in your program. A dialog box for choosing the file(s) to e-mail will appear.
7. Use the Look In list to navigate to the folder holding the picture(s) to send.

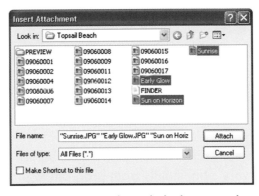

FIGURE 10.1 You can select multiple photos to send as files attached to an e-mail message.

8. Select one or more photos to attach (see Figure 10.1). Click to select a single photo, or use Shift+click or Ctrl+click to select multiple adjacent or nonadjacent photos, respectively.
9. Click on Attach, Insert or the applicable button in the dialog box. The dialog box will close, returning you to the message window. The attached picture file(s) will be listed as attachments in a text box or displayed as icons in the message body area. See Figure 10.2.
10. Click Send. Your e-mail program will transfer the message to its Outbox.
11. Click Send/Recv or choose the equivalent button or command in your e-mail program. Your e-mail program will connect to the Internet, if needed, and send the message with the picture files attached.

10

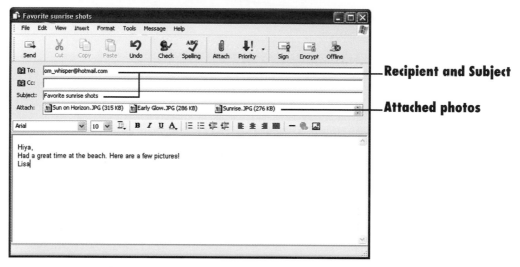

FIGURE 10.2 An e-mail message with picture files attached.

From Photo Editing or Album Software

You may find it more convenient to e-mail a particular photo right when you're working on it in your photo editing or photo album software. In particular, this method enables you to preview images or make any needed corrections before sending. The commands and methods for sending vary significantly from program to program, so the following steps provide an overview of the procedure to follow:

❶ Select the photo to send, either by opening the image as the current image in your image editing software or by clicking on the image in the photo library or an album in the photo album software.

❷ Choose the command for sending the message:

♦ In image editing software, you typically choose File, Attach to E-mail or File, Send. Windows will open a new e-mail message window from your e-mail program, with the active file inserted as a file attachment. From there, address and send the message as just described.

♦ In album software, click on the command or button (such as an Email or Share button) for starting an e-mail. Either the selected image(s) will be inserted as a file attachment for a regular e-mail as just described or a screen will appear to prompt you for message information. If the latter occurs, follow the rest of these steps.

NOTE

Some programs may ask whether you want to compress the file to a smaller size for the e-mail.

③ Enter your e-mail address in the From: text box.
④ Enter the recipient's e-mail address in the To: text box.
⑤ Enter the message subject in the Subject: text box.
⑥ Type the message contents in the Message body area of the message window.
⑦ When you've finished creating the message (see Figure 10.3), click Send. The album software will connect to the Internet and send the photo, using its own mailing service if required.

NOTE

Some of your friends or family members may not know how to save picture files attached to an e-mail message that they've received. Let them know that they need to select the received message, typically by clicking the message in the Inbox list. Then they can either choose File, Save Attachments or click on the paper clip icon beside the message header and then click Save Attachments. Use the Browse button in the Save Attachments dialog box to determine the disk and folder location for the saved files, and then click Save.

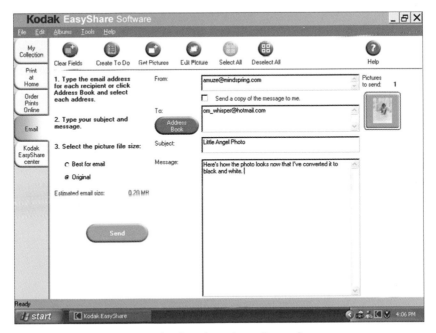

FIGURE 10.3 Preparing to e-mail a photo from photo album software.

10

REALLY INSTANT PHOTO SENDING VIA IM

If you're the parent of an adolescent or teenager or work in an environment that's reasonably tech savvy, then you've probably heard about or seen *Instant Messaging* (IM) in action. IM enables users to "chat" online by typing and sending brief messages. Because the messages travel quickly (as quickly as the messaging service and respective Internet connections will allow), IM works and feels much more immediate than e-mail.

Recent IM systems and software have evolved to provide numerous additional capabilities, including the capability to send files such as photos to a person with whom you're chatting. This process can work even more quickly and directly than e-mail. However, it has a few requirements beyond those for e-mail:

✦ Both the sender and recipient must have the software for the IM service installed.

✦ Both must have a logon for the service and have designated the other person as a chat buddy.

✦ Both must be logged on to the IM system to initiate a send.

Once those conditions apply, either chatter can follow these steps (generally) to send a photo:

1. The chatters should start messaging one another.

2. Click the Send Files button.

3. Use the Send a File dialog box to select the file to send. The selected photo will appear in the IM program window (see Figure 10.4).

4. The file recipient must accept the file send. For example, in the latest version of MSN Messenger, the recipient must press Alt+C or click on the Accept link. The file will transfer. When the transfer finishes, the sender will receive a "transfer complete" message in the IM window. The recipient will see a "successfully received" message, along with a link to the hard disk location where the messaging software stored the received file.

FIGURE 10.4 Preparing to send a photo via IM software.

Including a Photo in a Web Page

If you like to create custom Web pages to share information online with friends and family, including photos invites the page viewer to be part of your recent life experiences. For example, a friend of mine who married set up a Web page with the best photos from the wedding so that guests and others could log on and enjoy the happy event all over again.

While an exhaustive review of how to prepare Web graphics would go too far for this book, there are some general guidelines you may find helpful. For example, you will never want to insert a digital photo as shot by the camera into a Web page. Original files typically are too large and are not optimized for Web download. Use image editing software such as Adobe Photoshop Elements or Jasc Paint Shop Pro to reduce the image dimensions and quality. Usually, an image size of 320×240 pixels will be the *largest* size to place on a Web page, and you may choose to use even smaller sizes for thumbnail images.

In addition, you may want to convert the graphics to another file type. Typically, insert either a JPEG or GIF image on a Web page. If you've cropped the image in an irregular shape and want it to remain transparent, you will need to choose the GIF format. If you want to preserve a photo's realistic look but improve its download speed, you can choose the JPEG format, choose a lower quality setting, and set the image to use *interlaced* or *progressive* downloading.

With *interlaced* or *progressive* downloading (*interlacing*), the image can appear in the Web page after partially downloading. The Web page visitor can thus see the Web page image faster.

10

Fortunately, even more entry level image editing programs provide you help with creating images optimized for the Web. Rather than you having to apply various commands and conversions and guess at the outcome, you can use an optimizer feature to choose Web conversion settings all in one location and see a side-by-side preview of the image before and after optimization.

To start the process, you open the file to convert and then choose a single command. For example, in Adobe Photoshop Elements 2.0, choose File, Save for Web. In Jasc Paint Shop Pro 8, choose File, Export and then choose either the JPEG Optimizer or GIF Optimizer command. The window for optimizing the image will appear.

Choose the desired file format, size, and quality settings. Check the preview of the optimized image to make sure it still looks adequately attractive, as shown in Figure 10.5. (For example, if you reduce a GIF image to use too few colors, it will take on an unappealing blocky appearance.) The bottom section of the preview for the optimized file also typically includes statistics about the optimized file, such as the new file size and estimated download time. Review these statistics to ensure they meet your criteria. When everything looks good, click on OK or Save to finish the conversion.

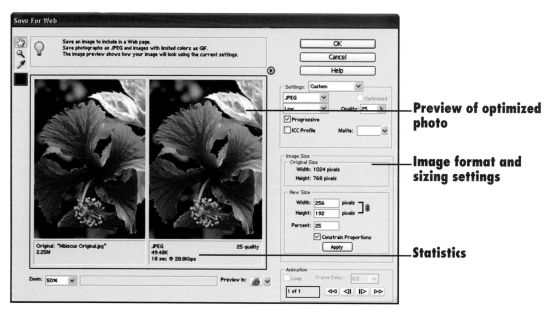

Preview of optimized photo

Image format and sizing settings

Statistics

FIGURE 10.5 Before including an image in a Web page, use image editing software to optimize the image format.

When prompted (typically by a Save Optimized As dialog box), specify a new name and save location for the optimized file. The software will close the dialog boxes both for saving and converting the file.

Once you've saved the optimized file, you can use your Web page development or word processing program to insert it in the page just as you would any other graphic. You can resize and format the inserted graphic file as needed, add a border, add a caption, and so on. Figure 10.6 shows the image from Figure 10.5 inserted into a Web page.

When you upload the finished Web page to your Web space provided by your Internet service provider (ISP) with your Internet account, be sure to upload the folder of images for each Web page. Otherwise, the page will load without the images in place. Generally, you will use an FTP utility program to transfer the files to a particular location online. Consult your ISP to learn more about the process for transferring and setting up Web pages on your account.

FIGURE 10.6 The optimized image placed on a Web page.

> **TIP**
>
> If you want to enable your friends and family members to still be able to download your full size images, create a preview page with a thumbnail of each image. Link each thumbnail to a second Web page on which you've inserted the full-sized image. From there, your friends and family can right-click the image and choose Save Picture As.

Setting Up an Online Photo Gallery

An online photo gallery is a Web location that shows a group of photos that you specify.

If you create your Web photo gallery using photo album software or an online service, during the process you will automatically e-mail persons with whom you want to share the gallery. When they view the Web gallery, they will be able to browse through the photos (see Figure 10.7) and order prints of the photos.

FIGURE 10.7 This online photo gallery was created using Adobe Photoshop Album, which by default works along with the Shutterfly.com online site for sharing photos online.

Using an album program or online service to create a Web photo gallery typically involves the following steps, although not necessarily in this order:

1. Log on to the online service or start the album software.
2. Select the photos or album that you want to share as a gallery.
3. Choose the command or button for starting the gallery.
4. Specify the names and e-mail addresses of recipients whom you want to invite to view the photo gallery.
5. Click Send or otherwise complete the gallery creation process.

If you want to create a Web photo gallery that's independent of an online service but don't want to create the gallery from scratch, you can use image editing software such as Adobe Photoshop Elements 2.0. This program creates a main Web page with image thumbnails. When the viewer clicks on a particular thumbnail, a Web page with a larger version of the image appears.

If you're using Photoshop Elements to create a Web gallery, it will create a main Web page named index.htm. In addition, it will create a subfolder named \pages\ to hold all the linked Web pages to show the individual images, as well as a subfolder named \images\ to hold copies of the original image file.

The steps for creating a Web gallery in Photoshop Elements follow. Of course, this process will vary in other programs offering this functionality.

1. Place all the image files that you want to appear in the Web gallery in a single folder on your hard disk.
2. Start Photoshop Elements.
3. Choose File, Create Web Photo Gallery.
4. Using the choices in the Web Photo Gallery dialog box (see Figure 10.8), choose the settings for the photo gallery, including a gallery style, the folder holding the images to include in the gallery (Browse), and the destination where the finished gallery files will be stored.

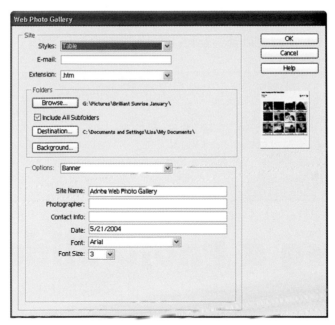

FIGURE 10.8 Adobe Photoshop Elements enables you to create a Web gallery of images that you can share on the Internet.

5. Click OK. Photoshop Elements will create the gallery Web pages and display a preview of the gallery, as shown in Figure 10.9. The gallery preview has all navigation elements in place, such as buttons for moving between pages and links between each thumbnail and its corresponding page with the original image. You can test the links before uploading the gallery files to your Web space.

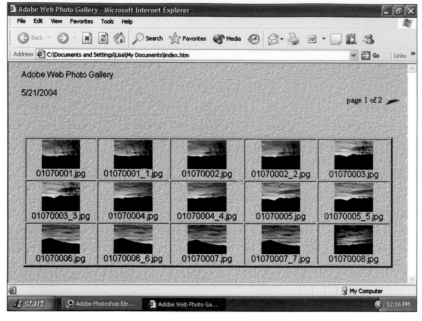

FIGURE 10.9 Preview the Web photo gallery before uploading it to the Web.

TIP

There also are online services that enable you to store your photos online, organize them into albums, and share them with other users. The Sacko online service (http://www.sacko.com) is free, but other such services charge a monthly or annual fee. These fee-based sites include Funtigo Deluxe (http://www.funtigo.com), PhotoSite (http://www.photosite.com), and SmugMug (http://www.smugmug.com).

Creating a Photo Slideshow

A photo slideshow enables you to select a group of photos and show them onscreen one at a time. In some album software, such as the Kodak EasyShare program, the slide-show plays immediately after you create it, but it is not saved as an independent file.

Using other software, including Adobe Photoshop Album and Adobe Photoshop Elements, you can save the slideshow as a PDF file (Adobe's Portable Document Format file format) that you can then e-mail to a friend or family member (if the file is small enough) or burn to a CD-R for sharing. To play back the slideshow, double-click on the PDF file in a Windows XP folder window. (In the case of a slideshow created in Adobe Photoshop Album, you also have to click on a play button in the initial screen that appears in Adobe Acrobat Reader.)

Creating a slideshow takes only minutes. For example, in Photoshop Album, you select the photos to include and then click on the Create button. The Create Slideshow dialog box (see Figure 10.10) will appear. Drag the pictures to a new order, if needed, and then click the Create Slideshow button. In the Save as PDF dialog box, choose a Size and Quality option, and then click OK. Specify a name and save location in the Export PDF As dialog box, and then click OK.

CAUTION

By default, most PDF slideshows do not save images at full resolution, so this is not the method to use to send images when the recipient may want to order prints. If that's the case, e-mail the images instead or share them as a Web photo gallery.

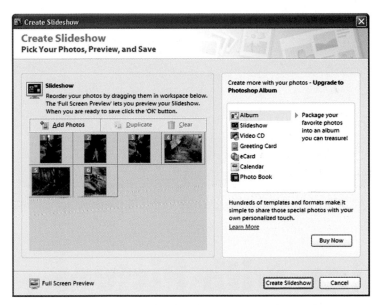

FIGURE 10.10 Creating a PDF slideshow that you can e-mail or send on CD-R for playback.

In Photoshop Elements, the process is equally easy. Choose File, Automation Tools, PDF Slideshow. Use the Browse button in the PDF Slideshow dialog box that appears to add files to the slideshow, and use the Choose button to specify a name and save location for the finished PDF file. Set Slide Show Options such as whether the slideshow should loop (repeat), and then click OK.

To start a PDF slideshow, double-click on its PDF file icon in Windows.

Figure 10.11 shows the first slide (image) in a slideshow of pictures taken after an ice storm. If you created the slideshow from album software, the slideshow might include a bar with buttons that you can use to advance the slides. Depending on how you created a PDF slideshow, the slides might advance automatically, or you can click with the mouse or press the spacebar to move through the images. In either kind of slideshow, you can press Esc to stop playback.

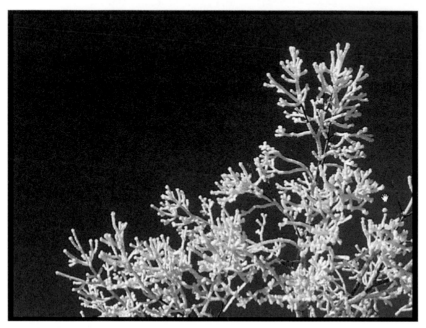

FIGURE 10.11 In most cases, when you create a slideshow, its images appear at full-screen size.

Working with Picture Phone Images

Today's mobile phones have caused a controversy due to inappropriate use by some folks (such as kids taking pictures of school materials in order to cheat on tests), but these cameras offer a fun and fast way to snap and share pictures. Whether you encounter a funny scene when you're walking down the street and want to share it or want to preserve a record of a fender bender on the spot, a picture phone or camera phone will do just what you need (see Figure 10.12). You can share picture phone images either with other mobile phone users who also have picture phones or by e-mailing the pictures from your picture phone.

FIGURE 10.12 This Motorola v400 picture phone features a bright screen and easy picture-taking capabilities.

If you're considering purchasing a picture phone to expand your digital photo capabilities, there are a few points to consider:

✦ Picture phones are the top of the line as of this writing, so one may cost you $200 or so plus a plan commitment, even if you are upgrading with your existing mobile service provider.

✦ To be able to share the picture phone pictures via phone or e-mail, you typically have to upgrade your phone service to include multimedia messaging and/or Internet and e-mail access, where available. This will typically add several dollars per month to your phone plan charges. In addition, any recipient who wants to receive picture messages must have a phone and an account capable of multimedia messaging. Finally, if you want to e-mail messages from the phone, your wireless provider may require you to complete an additional online signup process to enable e-mail transfer.

✦ Current picture phones take images at rather low resolution: 640 × 480. They offer only limited capabilities to adjust brightness and zoom, and of course most have no built-in flash. Don't plan on using a current picture phone as your main digital camera. Future picture phones will almost certainly offer increasingly better picture quality and functionality.

10

✦ Current picture phones offer limited storage space for photos. For example, the model shown in Figure 10.12 has only 5 MB of internal storage for all multimedia content, including wallpapers, screensavers, ringtones, games, and pictures taken with the camera. If you plan to use your phone's picture-taking capabilities regularly, choose a phone with greater storage or invest in a data transfer cable (about $30 extra) so you can more easily transfer images to your computer.

CAUTION

And of course, network coverage matters. My brand-spankin'-new picture phone gets a bit finicky at times when I try to send picture e-mails.

With all that being said, most digital camera phones make it relatively easy to shoot a picture (steps will vary from phone to phone, however):

1. Press the button or command to start the picture-taking process.
2. Hold the phone so that the camera lens points at the picture subject; use the LCD preview to compose the picture.
3. Use the controls for adjusting brightness and zoom, if any.
4. Press the button for capturing the picture.
5. Preview the picture in the LCD, then press the button for storing the picture.

Once you've stored a picture on the camera, you can use the camera's menu system to work with the pictures. For example, on my camera, I open the main menu, choose Multimedia, and then choose Pictures. From there, I can use the arrows on the rocker/scroller button to scroll down to a picture and select it for preview. Once the picture's onscreen, I can press the main menu button again and choose whether to send the picture to another person's phone or e-mail address (see Figure 10.13) or otherwise work with the picture.

If your phone doesn't offer you the capability to sync with your computer via a wireless or USB connection (you may have to purchase the transfer cable separately), you will need to e-mail pictures to your own e-mail address and then save them to your computer's hard disk in order to edit or print them.

FIGURE 10.13 This picture phone picture was sent via e-mail.

TIP

If your picture phone has Bluetooth or infrared file transfer capabilities, you may be able to print pictures directly from the camera using a retail kiosk. For example, pharmacy chain CVS (http://www.cvs.com) offers this capability at the kiosks in some of its stores. The process involves transferring the images from the phone to the kiosk. From there, you can order prints as you would when printing from digital camera storage media.

10

11

Transforming Photos into Keepsakes

In this chapter:

◆ Learning about online photo services

◆ Converting your photos into various keepsakes

◆ Using software to do it yourself

I f you want to have a lot of photo prints made, your inkjet may not be the best choice. You may instead opt to use an online photo printing service, which can make prints of your images in a variety of sizes, as well as creating other keepsakes from your digital images. This chapter introduces you to online printing services, showing you some of the great projects you can create.

Exploring Online Photo Services

When digital photography started booming, a number of services that made prints from negatives established online stores to make prints from digital images. They have been joined by a number of new outfits, as well. You can now choose from a number of online printing services that offer a variety of features and products.

Typically, you can become a member of an online photo printing service for free by completing a simple signup procedure that includes establishing a sign in ID and password. Once you've joined, you can upload your photos to the service's storage server; this may require first downloading and installing a software add-on from the service (especially if you want to upload multiple photos at a time). Typically, each batch of photos you upload is stored as a separate virtual "film roll." Many services enable you to create and store photos in virtual albums and change the order of photos by dragging them around in the album.

Once your prints are on the server, you can start ordering prints and having fun. Print prices are modest, ranging from $.22 to $.39 for a 4 × 6 print. Prices for larger print sizes are equally affordable. These online services also offer a variety of other services as well, including editing photos and adding borders, sharing and e-mailing photos, creating slideshows and ordering them on DVD, and creating specialty items such as greeting cards from your photos.

TIP

Some photo services give you free prints just for signing up. For example, when I joined Shutterfly, I received 15 free prints. Typically, the service will send you an e-mail confirming how to order your freebies. Many services also offer sales from time to time, giving you discount pricing for a certain timeframe or for a certain number of prints.

Table 11.1 lists the most popular online services, so you can start visiting their Web sites to compare services and select one or more that you'd prefer to use.

TABLE 11.1 Online Photo Services

Name	URL
Club Photo	http://www.clubphoto.com
dotPhoto	http://www.dotphoto.com
ez prints	http://www.ezprints.com
ImageStation	http://www.imagestation.com
Kodak Picture Center Online	http://picturecenter.kodak.com
Ofoto	http://www.ofoto.com
PhotoAccess	http://www.photoaccess.com
PhotoWorks	http://www.photoworks.com
Shutterfly	http://www.shutterfly.com
Snapfish	http:/www.snapfish.com
Wal-Mart	http://www.walmart.com, click Photo Center link

NOTE

If you're a Mac user, the iPhoto 4 album software provides photo print and book printing through Kodak. Use the Order Prints or Order Book tool to start the ordering process.

NOTE

Some photo album programs have arrangements to work directly with the online photo services. For example, the command for ordering prints in Adobe Photoshop Album 2.0 enables you to connect to the Shutterfly or Photo Access Print Processing service to upload and order your photos.

11

Photo Prints

It takes only a few minutes to order prints of your photos from an online print service. Generally, the process works as follows:

1. Open a photo roll or album and select the uploaded photo(s) to reprint.
2. Choose the command or button for ordering prints.
3. Specify the print size and quantity.
4. Specify whether you want color prints or want the images converted to black-and-white or sepia, if available.
5. Choose whether the service should apply any additional processing, such as zooming, color correction, or white borders.
6. Choose the desired print finish, typically either glossy or matte.
7. Complete the checkout process, specifying a shipping method and providing payment information.

Some online photo services also enable you to create prints with a decorative border, as shown in Figure 11.1. Generally, you can select the photo to which you want to add the border, select the border, and complete the order by specifying the number of prints desired and then checking out.

FIGURE 11.1 Adding a decorative border to a print.

Usually you'll receive your prints in a week or so, depending on the shipping method you select.

Photo Greeting Cards

You also can share your favorite photo by having it printed as a photo greeting card. Because they're personal and priced competitively with generic cards from the drugstore or card shop, they've become quite popular during the Christmas/Hanukkah/Kwaanza/New Year's/holiday season.

The process for creating and ordering your custom greeting card will typically resemble ordering prints, depending on the photo service you're using:

1. Open a photo roll or album and select the uploaded photo to use for the card.
2. Choose the command or button for creating greeting cards.
3. Select a season/holiday/occasion and design category.
4. Choose the design elements for the card, such as the photo border, greeting style, and background. You will see a preview of your card, like the one in Figure 11.2.
5. Enter the message and signature to include on the card.
6. Preview the card text, and edit it if needed.
7. Specify the number of cards you want.
8. Complete the checkout process, specifying a shipping method and providing payment information.

FIGURE 11.2 Creating a holiday greeting card online.

Mugs to Mousepads

Some online services enable you to order a variety of different novelty items with your photo. While the availability of novelty choices will vary from site to site, PhotoAccess seems to have the best selection, so I'll use it as an example. Table 11.2 lists the special items you can have printed via the PhotoAccess service as of this writing.

You can imagine how much fun you can have creating and ordering items like these. Grandma would love a refrigerator magnet with a picture of the baby. Hubby won't feel as lonesome traveling for business with a picture of you and the kids on his luggage tag. Mom would love a jewelry box or tile featuring a favorite photo of all her kids.

Shop around from service to service to find the special items that you want, and get ready to thrill your friends and family members with personalized gifts. To start the process, just select the type of item to order and follow the onscreen directions for selecting the photo to print and completing the order.

TABLE 11.2 Photo Print Novelties Available from PhotoAccess*

Item	Price (Without Shipping)
8" × 10" photo puzzle	$11.95
Trivet with photo tile	$24.95
Mousepad	$11.50
Mug (13.5 oz.)	$16.95
Photo tile (4.25" square)	$9.99
Photo tile (6" square)	$16.99
T-shirt	$16.95
Wooden jewelry box with photo tile	$47.95 and up
Other novelties (desk clock, keychain, luggage tag, photo coasters, fridge magnets)	$6–20

Availability and prices as of 5/15/04

Calendars and Posters

You might like to reproduce your best photos in the calendar or poster format. Then, you can enjoy your work as you track your schedule, or add a nice frame and decorate your home or office.

Depending on your online provider, calendars may come in different sizes (12" × 7", 10" × 14", or 12" × 18"), with prices starting at $20 or so. Sometimes you can choose to create an 18-month calendar or a 12-month calendar. You also will be able to choose the starting date (month and year) for the calendar. During the calendar creation process, you will select an uploaded photo for each page of the calendar (12 or 18), as well as a cover photo. After specifying a cover title (see Figure 11.3) and design if available, you can preview the calendar pages and then complete your order.

> **TIP**
>
> When it comes to calendars and photo borders, it pays to check out a few different online services to see which design choices are available.

FIGURE 11.3 Enjoy a new photo every month by creating a calendar.

Some online providers offer very large prints, which they may refer to as posters, poster-sized prints, or large format prints. These are usually prints 16" × 20" and larger, with prices starting at $18 or so. The process for ordering poster-size prints usually resembles ordering regular prints, but there's one big difference. You need a high-resolution image to yield quality large prints. A 2-megapixel image will look good only at print sizes up to 5" × 7". For poster-size prints, you'll need an image above 4 megapixels.

The online service may even provide you a warning or advice about whether or not a particular picture file is suitable for printing in a large format. For example, in creating the order shown in Figure 11.4, I selected a 1,024 × 768 image (the low-res setting for my 3.3-megapixel camera). The site informed me that the photo resolution meant it was not suggested that I order prints of it in sizes above 5" × 7".

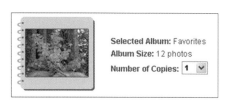

	Qty	Size	Okay to print?
	1	4x6	✓ Suggested
	0	5x7	✓ Suggested
	0	8x10	✗ Not suggested
Print preview	0	Wallet (4)	✓ Suggested
Remove	0	11x14	✗ Not suggested
	0	16x20	✗ Not suggested
	0	20x30	✗ Not suggested

Choose custom quantities for each picture

FIGURE 11.4 The online service may tell you that an image doesn't have adequate resolution for a poster-size print.

Photo Books

Many online services now offer the capability to create books from your photos. This convenient option eliminates the need for you to assemble photos into albums on your own. Photo books make great gifts, especially when created to commemorate a special event such as a wedding or a baby's first months. Depending on the online service you use, you may be able to order photo books in one of the following three formats:

◆ **Keepsake book, snapbook, or brag book.** This format typically means a mini spiral-bound book with one photo per page, as illustrated in Figure 11.5. You can purchase one of these books for a modest price. For example, Shutterfly offers a 5" × 7" snapbook with 11–20 pages for $11.99. You often can choose different designs to enhance the book pages, as well.

Selected Album: Favorites
Album Size: 12 photos
Number of Copies: 1

FIGURE 11.5 Order a mini keepsake book of a group of photos.

◆ **Fancy bound book.** Some online photo services offer a more upscale book format for your photos: a bound hardcover book that's professionally printed on glossy paper. This option is more rare, but some vendors such as ImageStation offer books starting at $29.99. You also can order a photo book if you're using iPhoto on a Mac. Figure 11.6 shows a 10-page, linen-bound photo book that I created to hold memories of a great vacation.

FIGURE 11.6 Professionally bound and printed photo books preserve your memories in style.

TIP

Another service called MyPublisher (http://www.mypublisher.com) specializes in printing photo books in both paperback and hardcover format. As of this writing, you could order a 20-page book with up to 80 photos for $9.95 (plus tax and shipping) on this site.

✦ **Scrapbook pages.** If your online photo service doesn't offer an actual bound book, it may enable you to compose and order scrapbook pages. Depending on the page design you select, you will be able to place one to four images on each page (see Figure 11.7). Select a design that fits the desired standard scrapbook page size: 9" × 12" or 12" × 12" sleeves. Each page you design and order will cost approximately $3–5.

FIGURE 11.7 Save time and get great results by designing your photo scrapbook pages online.

Using Software Instead of Online Services

If you still prefer to do it yourself rather than relying on an online service, you're not stuck if you're willing to invest a little money in some software. You can use project-oriented software along with specialty papers (such as T-shirt iron-on transfer paper) to create your own great photo projects. (Some image editing programs also enable you to create special projects like the ones described in this chapter.) Examples of the photo project programs are available at Dell.com:

✦ Art Explosion Greeting Card Factory Deluxe ($49.95), Photo Explosion Deluxe ($49.95), and Scrapbook Factory Deluxe ($39.95), Nova Development Corporation, http://www.novacorp.com for more information about software features.

✦ PrintMaster Platinum ($39.99) and PrintMaster Greeting Cards Deluxe ($17.95), Broderbund Systems, http://www.broderbund.com for more information about software features.

Check with Dell.com for additional programs and tools as they become available.

PART IV

Exploring Further Possibilities

12

Taking Better Photos

In this chapter:

- ◆ Observing the rule of thirds and framing your subject
- ◆ Using lighting to your advantage
- ◆ Exploring color and rhythm
- ◆ Photographing people
- ◆ Changing your point of view
- ◆ Capturing the right moment

You may now have reached your "awkward teenage years" in learning to use your digital camera. You're fairly comfortable using the controls, but you're not sure about the "magic" aspects of photography, such as how to discover and take a good picture. This chapter reveals traditional guidelines for composing better pictures, as well as other techniques that have worked well for me. Don't limit yourself to what you learn here, however. Build your own repertoire of tricks and tips as you build your personal portfolio of digital photographs.

Using the Rule of Thirds

Keeping the rule of thirds in mind helps you break away from taking "routine" photos with the subject centered in the shot. This technique works especially well with strong, well-defined subjects.

To use the rule of thirds when composing a photo, imagine that the scene you're viewing has gridlines dividing it into three rows and three columns. The gridlines define four points outside the center of the picture. Compose the picture so that the subject falls on or near one of those four points (see Figure 12.1). This offset placement enables the greater continuous background area to balance the strong subject.

Place the subject at one of these four points

FIGURE 12.1 Visualize a grid of three rows and three columns, and place your subject near one of the four resulting focal points.

Framing the Subject

Even if you don't like the formulaic feel of photos following the rule of thirds, you can still dramatize your photo subject by framing the photo with the subject off center. Let the nature of the scene guide you in placing the subject.

For example, Figure 12.2 shows my husband standing in front of a waterfall located near our home. I framed the photo with him at the bottom and the full height of the waterfall in view. This enabled me to include the many levels of the fall, as well as lending drama by showing its full drop. Similarly, you can look for backgrounds that nicely frame the subject for you.

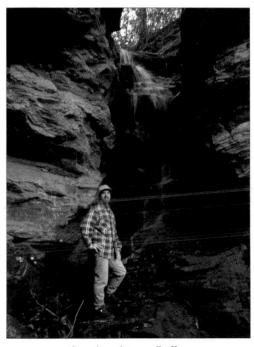

FIGURE 12.2 Place the subject well off center to provide scale and drama.

12

You may even choose to frame your photo so that the subject appears partially cropped out, as in Figure 12.3. This approach enables you to create unusual effects in your photos. In this example, the approach works because it highlights the color difference between the cosmos flower and the background. I could even place some text above the flower and then use the image as a logo or greeting card cover image. When shooting other subject matter, such as people or interiors, keeping certain content out of the frame may lend an air of mystery to the picture, provoking such questions as "What is she looking at over there?"

FIGURE 12.3 Extreme framing, even when the subject appears cropped, can have unexpected results.

Lighting the Subject

Chapters 3 and 4 ("Using Manual Camera Settings for Greater Control" and "Using Special Modes for Special Shots," respectively) covered a variety of topics related to working with the lighting settings available on digital cameras, such as flash, exposure compensation, and white balance settings. You also learned that you can use fill flash to expose deeply shadowed areas, and that you should avoid shooting in situations where backlighting might be a problem.

Here are additional tips for using lighting to your advantage when you're photographing your subject, particularly when working indoors:

✦ Always try to make sure the light source is behind you, particularly when shooting outdoors in bright sunlight. If that's not possible in an outdoor setting, then at least try to position yourself so that the sun falls at an angle between you and your subject.

✦ When you're working indoors, use the tools at hand to adjust the lighting to your advantage. For example, you may want to dim or turn off overhead lights and instead place a lamp at a particular location to provide softer, directional lighting. Tall floor lamps work particularly well for this purpose. If you're getting glare off particular objects, shut the window coverings or turn off the flash.

> **TIP**
>
> When an object has strong surface texture, you can emphasis the texture by lighting the object from the side.

✦ If you're further away from the subject, you may need more light, especially in dim indoor conditions. The light bouncing off of objects creates the image that we see, both through our eyes and through the camera viewfinder.

✦ Overcast days tend to be good for shooting outdoors. The lighting from an overcast sky softens the subject matter. The more shallow shadowing produced on an overcast day also enables you to capture details that might be buried in deep shadows when shot on a sunny day.

12

◆ When shooting at dusk, use shutter priority mode to choose a longer exposure, which may help improve the image (depending on how your camera then adjusts the aperture setting). Even better, if your camera offers a manual mode, choose it and select both a longer exposure and a smaller f-stop setting (for a wider aperture). As it gets darker, increase the exposure time to 30 seconds or more. You'll also probably want a tripod to eliminate shake. Even better, as dusk deepens, use the night scene mode if your camera offers one to have it adjust the exposure to the conditions.

◆ If you're shooting people a lot in evening conditions and don't like the harsh lighting created by your camera's flash, you may want to invest in a separate flash. That way, you can turn off the flash on the camera and direct the external flash to bounce off the wall or ceiling rather than hitting the subject head-on.

◆ Tune your eye to opportunities where the natural lighting creates a dramatic impact for you. For example, Figure 12.4 shows one of my favorite pictures that I've ever taken of my dog, Bo. Bright light streaming in through the window behind me cast dark, bold shadows at a diagonal angle. When he tilted his head to about the same angle, I snapped the shot. Outdoors, dappled sunlight (where tree leaves create small shadows among the light) can provide interesting, flattering lighting. Or, you may look for situations where you can capture strong beams of sunlight streaming from behind a cloud.

FIGURE 12.4 When I took this photo, bright light streaming in through the window created dramatic, deep shadows that perfectly highlighted Bo.

Using Color for Drama

Dark and light areas define the shapes you see in a photo, with high-contrast photos often appearing the most dramatic to the viewer. However, you also can look for strong contrasts between colors when composing an image.

For example, placing a brightly colored object against a white, gray, black, or neutral background will tend to make the object pop. Also, you can look for compositions where strong blocks of color balance one another in the photo, as in the example in Figure 12.5.

TIP

Red and yellow tones come across with more power than green and white. The photo in Figure 12.5 needed larger green areas, as composed, to offset the strong red roof.

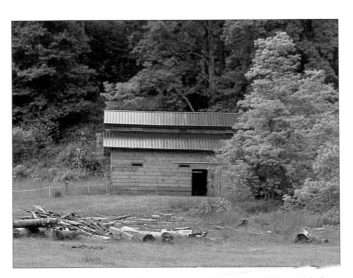

FIGURE 12.5 The strong reds and greens in this photo yield a simple but vivid composition.

12

Catching the Rhythm and the Pattern

Not every photo needs to have a strong focal point to interest the viewer. You can produce interesting photos by finding repeating elements that establish a pleasing rhythm or pattern.

For example, in Figure 12.6, the palm leaves create a rhythm as they whirl out from the central stalk. A row of fence pickets, dramatic siding on a building, dozens of icicles hanging from a gutter, kids or pets lined up in a row—look for such rhythmically oriented subjects and compose them dramatically in your shots.

Sometimes, pattern or texture will catch your eye, as in the example in Figure 12.7. The leaf itself isn't interesting, but the interplay of green shades gives it pattern and oomph. You might find interesting textures and patterns to photograph if you look closely at the bark on trees, a riverbank or beach area where water has flowed, or fields of flowers, for example.

FIGURE 12.6 Repeating elements such as the leaves radiating in this palm create a pleasing rhythm.

FIGURE 12.7 The pattern of colors in the leaf in the foreground attracted my attention.

Making People Look Good in Your Shots

Sometimes making people look great in your photos presents the biggest challenge. Not only is lighting key, but also the people you're photographing often look stiff and uncomfortable. The result: photos that look like mug shots or old-timey formal portraits.

If you slow down and take your time when shooting portraits, you can employ some simple techniques to create photos where the subjects look relaxed and terrific:

✦ Avoid simply posing people against a backdrop (unless you want a shot with a studio feel). Take pictures of your subject while doing something the subject loves or in a comfortable environment. Even if you're photographing a person who's standing or sitting, have him hold something in his hands to suggest an activity, such as reading glasses and a book. If you're taking a vacation photo, look for areas where the vista can frame the subject, as seen previously in Figure 12.2.

12

✦ Use soft lighting, soft focus, and a shallow depth of field (a low f-stop in aperture priority mode, so the subject looks focused, but the background looks soft) where possible. These techniques tend to downplay problematic features such as skin blemishes or wrinkles.

◆ Have the subject look away from you to capture a more flattering angle of the face. Even a slight side and downward tilt to the chin (but not so far down that a double chin develops) can create a more appealing appearance. If you *do* want the subject to look at you, have him angle the shoulders or body slightly to the left or right to make the pose less static.

◆ Harsh midday sun tends to produce deep shadows under the eyes, nose, and chin—not to mention causing the subject to squint and blink more. To correct this, move the subject into a slightly shaded area where the softer light will reduce shadows. For the same reason, sunrise and sunset are good times to shoot people; the light is soft and flattering at those times of day.

◆ Consider choosing a black-and-white or sepia mode if your camera offers one (or convert the photo later with image editing software). Eliminating color can eliminate unflattering problems such as uneven skin tone, so many people look better in black-and-white or sepia.

◆ When shooting indoors, the higher the light source, the deeper the shadows. Consider using the technique mentioned earlier in this chapter to light your subject better: Turn off overhead lights and position lamps to create lighting that's angled or comes from the side.

◆ Take a close look at the lighting if the subject is wearing glasses or a hat. When a subject wearing glasses looks directly at you, light tends to bounce off the glasses and create a large area of glare. Have the subject tilt the head up or look away at an angle to reduce the amount of glare bouncing off the glasses or, better yet, have the subject take off the glasses. On the other hand, a hat brim creates deep shadows on the subject's face. Use fill flash, add a light source coming from below and in front of the subject's face, or shoot the subject without the hat.

Figure 12.8 shows a portrait that meets a number of the above criteria. The subject (my brother) is engaged in something he loves (boating), is not looking directly at the camera (because he's driving the boat), has his sunglasses off, and is in shaded lighting under the boat awning rather than harsh sunlight.

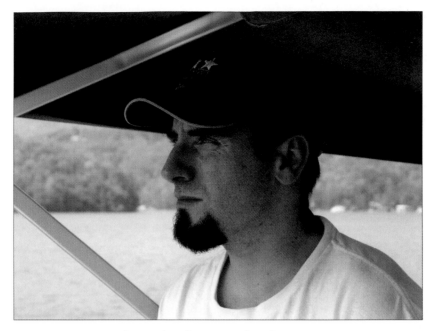

FIGURE 12.8 A portrait showing the subject engaged in a favorite activity seems more natural and spontaneous.

Working a Different Angle

The world doesn't exist just at your eye level. Different points of view and unusual angles can help you compose stronger pictures.

Don't restrict yourself to standing and taking pictures. For example, if you want to shoot children or pets, you might squat or lie down. You might kneel down to shoot an object close up or at a different angle. For example, to shoot the image shown in Figure 12.9, I knelt down to shoot the golden flowers through the fence, for a more interesting composition. Likewise, go above eye level to shoot your subject from above. Jump up in the bed of a pick-up truck or climb a ladder.

Also, look for unusual angles from which to shoot your subject. A photo taken from an oblique angle or with the camera rotated may improve dramatically upon a straight-on shot in the normal wide orientation.

12

FIGURE 12.9 Change your perspective by kneeling or climbing a ladder to take a photo.

Capturing the Moment

The shots you see in the newspaper and news magazines have interest because they convey a particular point in time or theme in addition to capturing the subject.

Don't be thrown if you're composing a picture and some person or object intrudes on the shot. For example, when I was framing a photo of the Grand Canyon from the south rim, my mom leaned out from behind a tree. Rather than being startled, I seized the moment and ended up with a shot of my mom (see Figure 12.10) that I just love.

By practicing, train yourself to find unusual, ironic, or exceptional situations. When you find one, shoot as many pictures as possible. For example, the dogs in Figure 12.11 caught my husband's eye. When he pointed them out to me, I *had* to take some shots of that ironic situation.

Above all, carry your camera with you everywhere, strive to stay loose, be spontaneous, and keep your eyes peeled for interesting shots.

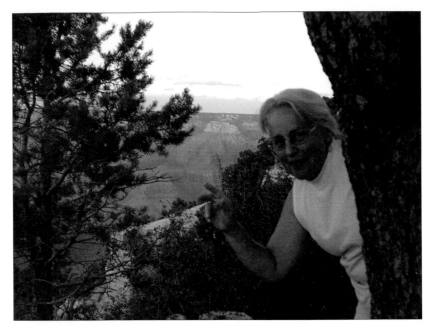

FIGURE 12.10 When my mom blocked my shot of the canyon, I took the photo anyway and got a great shot of her.

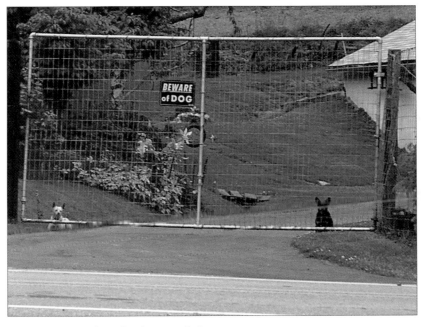

FIGURE 12.11 Watch out for these attack dogs!

12

13

Dealing with the Addiction?

In this chapter:

- ✦ Getting a little encouragement
- ✦ Keeping your shots organized
- ✦ Backing up your art
- ✦ Pushing your skills
- ✦ Following your muse

You've reached the end of the book but not the end of your experience with digital photography. Both your skills and the quantity of photos you've shot will improve steadily over time. Digital photography might even become your addiction. This chapter covers a few last topics to consider as your digital photography experience deepens.

Go Ahead and Shoot!

Chapter 1, "Choosing a Digital Camera," encouraged you to stock up on both large storage cards and batteries for your digital camera, to ensure that you can shoot as many pictures as needed for a given situation. You'll experience other practical benefits from shooting a lot of pictures, as well.

First of all, practice makes perfect. The more pictures you take and evaluate, the stronger your photographic "eye" will become. You will learn to frame the subject the way you prefer, identify the type of lighting you like to see, and choose just the right moment to snap the shot.

Secondly, you'll have a bit more insurance that you get the shot you want and have more shots to choose from when selecting the best. Figure 13.1 serves as a case in point. I took a series of sunrise photos on a rather chilly morning. This, one of the first photos shot, not only shows significant blur due to my shaking hands and a bit of

FIGURE 13.1 This shot was taken in haste, as illustrated by the uninteresting framing and blur from shaky hands.

autofocus trouble but also lacks interest in terms of the framing and the somewhat boring profile of the mountain.

Despite my initial failures, I kept shooting that morning. I tried slightly different locations, did a better job of bracing my camera hand (although I was still cold!), and just slowed down. As a result, I captured several better shots, such as the one in Figure 13.2. This latter shot includes more interesting cloud formations, and the lacy silhouette of the tree branches frames the shot in an interesting and unique way.

> **TIP**
>
> If you don't have a tripod but want to ensure a steadier hand when taking pictures, use an available hard, flat surface as a prop or brace. For example, if there's a half wall or countertop available, rest the elbow of the hand you're using to hold up the camera on that surface. If you're in a sitting or kneeling position, rest the elbow on your knee. Or, you can lean against a high wall or tree to better brace the camera. Some photographers even place a small bean bag on uneven surfaces like a car fender to help brace and level the camera.

FIGURE 13.2 This shot captures a better scene and eliminates the technical mistakes shown in Figure 13.1.

Finally, shooting a lot puts you in a better position to capture the right moment. If you take a shot or two and turn off your camera, you won't be able to power the camera back up soon enough to catch the great moment that happens 20 seconds later. Think of yourself as one of those sports photographers you see on TV. To get the great shot, they watch the game through the camera. Watch more of your surroundings through the lens, too, and you'll get better shots. (And have plenty of charged batteries on hand so that you can keep the camera turned on.)

13

A Little Organization, Please

You learned in Chapter 5, "Transferring Images to Your Computer," that digital cameras use a numbering system to name picture files. When you transfer the files to the computer directly via USB, the files retain their numeric names. Even if you use Windows XP to transfer files to your computer, it will assign all the files in a folder a similar name (Balboa001, Balboa002, and so on). Even with that bit of help from Windows XP, you're still left with trying to identify one photo from another based on a number.

Properly naming and organizing digital photos is one place where many users like me fall down on the job, and I pay for it. I've wasted a good deal of time searching for a particular shot on my hard disk. When I faced this problem with my film camera prints, I spent an entire day labeling the envelope for each set of prints with the date and subject of the photos. Suddenly, I could pluck any photo I needed from hundreds of others in a minute or so. Set the goal of always renaming your files and folders as soon as you transfer them to your PC. Consider Figure 13.3 as an example. You'll know *exactly* what's in the folder named Grand Canyon 9-30-03. In contrast, it's anyone's guess what's in the folder named 100_0930.

> **TIP**
>
> Don't let this happen to you: My photos are spread on the hard disks of a few different computers. If you're using multiple computers, are low on hard disk space, or simply want a centralized location to store your digital photo files, consider buying an external USB hard disk. For about $150, you can purchase an 80G USB 2.0 disk drive, providing you plenty of room for your shots. Because these hard disks are plug-and-play with Windows XP, you can easily unplug the disk from one computer and plug it into another, such as if you want to use the disk on your notebook computer rather than your desktop system.

Organizing and working with your photo files can help you in another way, as well. Virtually any camera today that captures JPEG images stores EXIF data in the JPEG file. This data preserves crucial details about how a picture was taken, including such facts as whether flash was used, what shutter speed and f-stop settings were used, and more.

FIGURE 13.3 Get in the habit of immediately assigning meaningful names to folders and digital images.

EXIF (EXchangeable Image File) data is interchange information that a digital camera stores with each image shot. This data includes statistics used to take the picture, such as the camera, resolution, shutter speed, exposure compensation, f-stop, flash, and more.

EXIF data can be crucial in helping you reproduce photos you like. You can review these settings for a favorite photo and reuse the settings to take later pictures of a similar subject with similar conditions. You can view EXIF information about a photo in either Windows XP or an image editing program, as illustrated in Figure 13.4.

◆ In a Windows XP folder window, right-click on the file and then click Properties. Click on the Summary tab in the Properties dialog box.

◆ In your image editing software, choose the command for viewing image information, such as File, File Info. Then choose the EXIF tab or section.

13

A Little Organization, Please 197

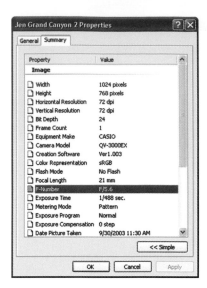
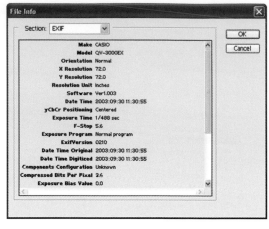

FIGURE 13.4 View EXIF data in Windows XP (left) or a photo editing program (right) to review the settings you used to take a favorite shot.

Back Up, Back Up, and Back Up Again

Backing up the data on your hard disk is another good piece of advice that too many of us ignore. If you don't have backup copies of your images and your hard disk fails, your photos will be lost forever.

You might think, "That's OK, I've printed them out on my inkjet printer, so I can always scan them again." Not so fast. Recent controversy centers on the question of how long inkjet photo prints will last. Even though inkjet printing and paper technology has improved dramatically in the last few years or so, inkjet printing technology has been around for only 15 years or so in all, so it's really unknown whether inkjet prints will last for decades as your film camera prints did.

Always have a plan B. Create a routine for backing up your digital photos. If you shoot a lot of pictures, backing up once a week is not excessive. If you work more infrequently, monthly backups can be appropriate.

Windows XP Home Edition does not include backup functionality. Still, you can create a backup by simply burning digital camera files to a CD-R or DVD-R, as described in the section called "Burning Your Photos to a CD-R in Windows XP" in Chapter 8, "Managing Your Photo Library."

If you want a more automated backup method, invest $75 or so in some backup software such as Dantz Retrospect (http://www.dantz.com), seen in Figure 13.5, to use along with your CD-R or DVD-R drive. (Using a tape backup drive for backups is less common today because CD-R speeds have improved, while CD-R media prices have dropped dramatically.) These programs enable you to schedule automatic backups, choose whether to perform a full or partial backup, and restore files. Download free trials of these programs to compare features.

NOTE

You don't have to back up all of your photos every time. You can choose to back up only the photo files that are new since your last backup. Backup software programs call this an *incremental backup*.

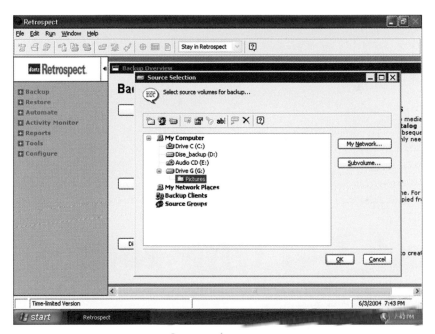

FIGURE 13.5 Backup software like Retrospect helps you automate backing up your picture files to CD-R. Here, a Pictures folder has been selected for backup.

For an all-in-one solution that also enables you to back up massive amounts of data (so you never have to worry about swapping a CD-R during a backup process), consider buying an external hard disk with pushbutton backup capabilities. Both Seagate and Maxtor make these drives, which literally back up your system when you press a button on the drive. These drives will set you back about $200 or so for a 120G USB 2.0/FireWire drive, but they offer great convenience and speed. These drives are

13

available through Dell.com, and you can learn more at their manufacturers' Web sites (http://www.seagate.com and http://www.maxtor.com).

Finally, if you prefer to pay as you go, have a broadband Internet connection, and want to have flexibility in backup capacity, consider an online backup service. For a monthly or yearly fee, these services provide you with a certain amount of storage space on their online servers. You can then back up your files to the service as desired, using software downloaded from the service if applicable. Here are a few examples of online backup services that you can check out:

- **@Backup (http://www.backup.com).** $49.95 per year for 50M.

- **Backmeupoffsite.com (http://www.backmeupoffsite.com).** Starts at $10.99 per month for 250M or $22.99 for 6G.

- **Connected TLM (http://www.connected.com).** $14.95 per month for 4G.

- **Xdrive (http://www.xdrive.com).** $10 per month for 500M.

TIP

Online backup services give the added benefit of being off site. Having a great pile of CD-R or DVD-R backups doesn't help if they're in your house when it burns down. If you really want security for your most treasured digital image files, consider burning them to CD-R or DVD-R and storing them in a safe deposit box.

Branch Out with Your Photo Skills

You can explore a variety of avenues to really push yourself to new skill levels with your digital photography and learn new techniques. Try out these types of activities to expand your experience:

- Look for volunteer opportunities where you can use your photography skills. You could get invaluable experience with photographing people. If a local charity will be holding a special event, volunteer to photograph the evening. Your church may need photographs for a newsletter or program. If your kids have joined a new sports league, the league may need someone to take team pictures. Check with volunteer coordinators at charitable organizations, church or league leaders, or local community volunteer agencies to find opportunities of interest.

NOTE

Mileage traveled for volunteer work may be tax deductible, depending on the tax status of the organization for which you're volunteering. Likewise, unreimbursed expenses (such as costs for inkjet photo paper) may be tax deductible. Consult your tax professional or IRS.gov to learn more.

◆ Enter photo contests or submit photos for critique. Most county fairs feature photo competitions, as do local art leagues. You may also find contests listed online at photography Web sites like www.popphoto.com. Contests typically restrict entrants to a particular theme or subject matter. Such constraints will compel you to find creative subjects and experiment with composition, lighting, and other aspects of the picture. Other Web sites such as www.photo.net allow members to upload photos for critique. Don't think of the resulting feedback as criticism. Think of it as valuable advice that you're getting for free from more experienced photographers.

◆ Your local paper may have a "photo corner" where it prints reader photo submissions that fit within a certain theme. For example, my local paper prints reader photos from exotic travel destinations. Not only will you see your photo in print, you'll also receive credit in the paper for your work.

CAUTION

Before you publish the picture of any human (or even pet) subject in any publication, be sure you have permission to do so. Historically, models have been given a token fee in return for agreeing to allow you to use their photo in publication. Today, permission requirements extend to photos published on Web sites, as well.

◆ Brainstorm your own photography projects, or combine photography with another favorite hobby. For example, you may want to focus on learning to take artistic photos of wildlife or plant life, which might require hiking and climbing. You might want to take pictures of your yard or the view from your house every month, and use them to create a calendar. If you love the night sky, some point-and-shoot cameras can shoot directly through the eyepiece of a telescope;

13

others require an adapter. Some projects might require you to purchase or put together other equipment, such as photo backdrops. But spending more time at the local photo shop and chatting with the customers and customer service reps there can help you tap into a lot of photo expertise in your local community.

◆ Check out your town's photo club. Most mid- to larger-size towns have photography clubs that meet regularly to discuss all types of photographic issues and techniques. Look for club listings in your local media to learn how to attend club meetings.

◆ Be your own photojournalist, and document an event or a project in your life. For example, if you're building your own house or shed (see Figure 13.6), you can document the process and share your progress with others. Behind-the-scenes shots of a wedding can be more treasured than the posed shots taken by a photographer.

◆ Be on the lookout for photography classes. Many community colleges and adult education centers offer open enrollment photography classes for a bargain fee. This provides a low-cost opportunity to learn more about photographic techniques, as well as providing a more structured way for you to learn.

FIGURE 13.6 Use your digital camera to document an event or a project in your life.

Break All the Rules

Experiment. A lot. Who cares if a few shots don't look good? All it costs you is a second or two spent deleting the boo-boo photo. If it gets results that you like, disregard all the advice laid out in the previous chapter. Use the wrong lighting. Ignore the rule of thirds. Pose your portrait subjects rather than working spontaneously.

You are the only and best judge of what appeals to you, and your tastes will evolve over time. Follow your artistic muse, and you will take the photos you love, whether you want to focus on still life photos, nature photos, animals, or people.

13

Glossary

Album. A specific collection of images selected from the library in photo album software.

Aperture or aperture size. The aperture is a diaphragm positioned along with the shutter between the lens and the sensor in a digital camera. The aperture is made of a number of pieces of thin material positioned in a circular formation so that they form a circular opening in the center. The aperture's parts move to change the size of the circular opening to admit more or less light while the shutter is open, much like the iris of an eye, resulting in a particular exposure. That's why an aperture is sometimes called an iris diaphragm.

Aperture priority. A picture-taking mode in which the user chooses the desired aperture setting (f-stop) while the camera controls the shutter speed.

Artifacts. Imperfections in a JPEG image due to the fact that JPEG compression involves discarding image data. Artifacts include halos (color leakage beyond the edges of objects) and jagged or blocky-looking areas in the background.

Auto focus. The default focus mode for most digital cameras, where the camera evaluates the subject distance to focus the lens.

Backlighting or backlit. When a strong light source comes from behind the subject so the subject looks dark. In backlit conditions, you should choose one of your camera's flash settings to provide fill flash or reposition the subject with relation to the light source.

Black-and-white (grayscale). An image that uses only gray tones from black to white, with no color hue.

Border. An effect you can apply around the edges of a digital image to make it more interesting. Some borders create an edge effect, such as splatters, around the edges of the photo. Others add a contrasting frame, such as one that looks like wood or metal, around the edges of the photo.

Brightness. The relative lightness or darkness in an image.

Burst mode (also called continuous mode). A picture-taking mode in which the camera automatically takes multiple consecutive shots (such as taking several shots in a 10-second period) to capture a subject in motion. This mode enables the photographer to catch unanticipated nuances in the action.

CD-R. A writable storage medium that resembles CD-ROM.

CD-R drive or burner. A disk drive that can write information to CD-R or CD-RW media.

Close-up mode. See *macro mode.*

Composing. Setting up a picture by making such decisions as placing the subject and lighting, zooming and focusing, and positioning the subject in the viewfinder or preview. Also called framing.

Contact sheet. A printout of multiple photos on a single page that presents each photo as a small thumbnail. Contact sheets can be made by photo labs or printed from photo album or image editing software. A contact sheet enables you to show a large number of photos to someone else for the purpose of selecting the best photos.

Contrast. The relative difference (light to dark) between the bright tones (highlights) and dark tones (shadows) in an image. An image with high contrast has very light highlights and very dark shadows.

Depth of field. Also known as the focus range, the range or distance within which the camera can focus with acceptable sharpness. While the lens focal length and distance from the subject play a role, aperture size probably does the most to determine the focus range in a picture.

Digital SLR. See *SLR.*

Dock. A device onto which you can place a digital camera to enable it to transfer images to a PC or charge the camera's battery pack. Some docks also include print capabilities.

Dpi (dots per inch). A measure of the resolution and quality of a printed image. The more dots per inch, the finer the size of each dot, and therefore the higher the print quality. Higher dpi values are better.

EXIF (EXchangeable Image File) data. Interchange information that a digital camera stores with each image shot. This data includes statistics used to take the picture, such as the camera, resolution, shutter speed, exposure compensation, f-stop, flash, and more.

Exposure. The amount of light allowed to pass through the camera lens to strike the film or sensor, based on various camera settings, to create an image.

Exposure bracketing. Taking photos of a subject at three or more similar f-stop settings (f/4, f/5.6, and f/8, for example) or three or more consecutive shutter speeds to ensure that an image with the desired exposure will be captured.

Exposure compensation. An automated camera feature that enables you to adjust exposure quickly to make a picture one or two steps lighter or darker.

G

f-stop. A value that indicates aperture size. f-stop settings are expressed like this: f/2, f/2.8, f/4, f/5.6, f/8, f/11, and so on.

Fill flash. In very bright lighting conditions or situations in which the subject is backlit, you would use at least some flash (the fill flash) to brighten the deep shadows so that the detail becomes visible in the picture.

Filmstrip view. A view for Windows XP file folders that shows a large thumbnail of each folder and image stored in the current folder. If a folder holds images, its thumbnail previews four of the images that it holds. The view arranges all the thumbnails in a strip along the bottom of the folder window. Clicking on an image in the strip displays a larger preview of the image in the window.

Filter. 1. A special, removable lens cover added to a camera lens to apply a specific effect to the light entering the camera. For example, some filters use tints to highlight certain light colors in the finished image or screens to create a starburst effect. 2. A special effect that you can apply to an image using image editing software (for example, a watercolor effect).

Focus lock. A camera feature that enables the user to focus the camera on an object, lock the current focus setting (by pressing the shutter halfway down and holding it in that position), and then direct the camera at another subject to take its picture instead.

Frame. See *border*.

Freehand selection tool. See *Lasso tool*.

Hue. The colors contained in an image. Use image editing software to adjust the hue, making the image redder, for example.

Infinity mode. A focus mode that helps the camera focus on very distant objects.

Inkjet printer. A form of color printer that creates a printed image by spraying droplets of ink on paper. Most recent inkjet printer models are capable of printing photo quality images.

Interlaced (progressive). An image saved for the Web in such a way that it can appear when partially downloaded, giving the appearance of a faster download.

Landscape mode. A picture-taking mode in which the camera ensures that everything from the foreground to distant objects is focused.

Lasso tool. A tool you can use to make irregularly shaped selections in an image editing program.

Library. All the photos stored on your computer—or more specifically, imported into a photo album or catalog program.

Macro mode. A lens focus mode that enables a digital camera to shoot pictures of subjects as close as 2.5 inches (or even closer, depending on the camera mode) from the camera.

Manual focus mode. A mode on some digital cameras that enables the user to manually focus the image, rather than using the camera's auto focus mode.

My Pictures. A folder created for each Windows XP user, intended as the central place for organizing digital images.

Optimized. An image saved with a proper format, color palette, interlacing, and other settings that best prepare it for use on a Web page. Many image editing programs offer the ability to preview optimization settings.

Orientation. Refers to whether an image is composed vertically (tall or portrait orientation) or horizontally (wide or landscape orientation).

Overexposed. An image in which camera settings permitted too much light through the lens to make the picture, resulting in an image that has heavy shadows that obscure all the detail—or even an image that's totally washed out.

Panning. In an image editing program, moving a selector to determine what portion of a zoomed-in image remains visible in the image window. When taking a picture, moving the camera to follow the action.

Panorama mode. A picture-taking mode that enables you to shoot a sequence of overlapping photos that you can later combine into a single panorama image using image editing software.

Photo album software. This type of program enables you to import all your pictures into a digital library and manage your pictures from that central location. You can organize images from the library into separate albums or collections, print images, order prints, and more.

Picoliter. A unit of measure for ink drop size on inkjet printers. Smaller picoliter values indicate finer print quality.

Picture package. A printout that repeats a single image in multiple sizes on a single page to use paper efficiently.

Pixel. Short for **Pic**ture **El**ement, a single dot of color information in a digital image or printed image.

G

Portrait mode. A picture-taking mode that fuzzes the background but shows the subject in crisp detail to emphasize the subject.

Ppi (pixels per inch). A measure of the resolution of a digital image. The higher the value, the finer the picture and the larger size at which it can be printed. Ppi also can refer to a monitor's resolution.

Print resolution. The quality indicator for printed output, measured in dpi. The higher a printer's maximum resolution, the higher-quality prints it can produce.

Red-eye. An unnatural red or green glow in the eyes of a photographed human or animal, caused by flash lighting bouncing off the back of the eye.

Red-eye flash mode or red-eye reduction mode. A flash mode on a digital camera that attempts to prevent red-eye, typically by firing the flash twice.

Rotate. To reorient an image in either the clockwise or counterclockwise direction.

Rule of thirds. A method for composing a photo. Imagine that the scene you're viewing has gridlines dividing it into three rows and three columns. The gridlines define four points outside the center of the picture. Compose the picture so that the subject falls on or near one of those four points. This offset placement enables the greater continuous background area to balance the strong subject.

Saturation. The purity of a color based on the amount of gray mixed with the actual hue.

Self-timer. A camera feature that enables the photographer to compose the shot and then jump into the picture during a delay period (2 or 10 seconds, for example) after pressing the shutter.

Sensor. The device in a digital camera that reads the light photons entering the camera and converts them to electrical charges so that the image can be stored. Most digital cameras use either a CCD or CMOS sensor.

Sepia. A special brownish photo tint meant to make an image look old. Sepia images look softer than black-and-white images. Most image editing programs have commands for converting a color image to sepia.

Shutter priority. A picture-taking mode in which the user controls exposure by choosing the desired shutter speed, while the camera automatically chooses the f-stop setting for correct exposure.

Shutter speed. The amount of time the shutter stays open after you press the shutter button to allow light onto the camera sensor. Shutter speeds are expressed in seconds and fractions of seconds, with a 1/60 shutter speed meaning that the shutter will be open for one-sixtieth of a second.

SLR (Single Lens Reflex). Refers to 35mm cameras where the lens functions for both viewing and taking pictures, yielding truer photo results. High-end digital cameras with removable lenses are often called digital SLRs.

Sport mode. A picture-taking mode that automatically selects a fast shutter speed for making an in-motion subject look still (reducing blur) in a digital image.

Storage card (storage medium). A card inserted into a digital camera to expand its image storage capabilities. Storage card types include CompactFlash, SmartMedia, Secure Digital, MMC (MultiMediaCard), Memory Stick, and xD Picture Card.

Thumbnails view. A view for Windows XP file folders that shows a large thumbnail of each folder and image stored in the current folder. If a folder itself holds images, its thumbnail previews four of the images that it holds.

Underexposed. An image in which camera settings permitted too little light through the lens to make the picture, resulting in an image with flat, dull tones that is too dark overall.

White balance. An exposure correction feature that sets the brightest part of the image to white (eliminating tints that can occur from fluorescent or incandescent lighting, for example) and adjusts other tones accordingly. This can be either an automatic or a manual setting.

Zoom. The camera's ability to change the focal length of the lens so that the picture will appear to have been taken closer to or farther from the subject. With optical zoom, the camera actually changes the focal length of the lens. With digital zoom, the camera uses interpolation to calculate image information as if the actual (optical) zoom had been changed.

G

Index

A

hats, subjects wearing, 188
hobbies, combining, 201–202
holiday cards. *See* greeting cards
horizon, taking pictures of, 181

I

IBM Microdrive, 14
   printing directly from, 146
icons
   for close-up mode, 53
   for flash modes, 38–39
   for landscape mode, 54
   for night mode, 58
image editing programs. *See also*
     borders and frames; filters
   artifacts, removal of, 93
   black-and-white, converting to, 107–108
   borders, adding, 102–104
   choosing, 82–83
   collages, creating, 110–111
   color, correction of, 95–97
   cropping images with, 84–86
   duotone images, creating, 108
   EXIF information, viewing, 197–198
   fill lighting, adding, 88–90
   filters, applying, 100–102
   grayscale images, converting to,
     107–108
   panoramas, creating, 55, 110–111
   printing photos from, 135–138
   red-eye removal with, 87–88
   rotating images with, 84–86
   scratches, removing, 93–94
   sepia images, creating, 108–110
   sharpening images with, 90–93
   softening images with, 90–93
   spots, removing, 93–94
   text, combining photos with, 105–106
   tone, correction of, 95–97
   for Web page photos, 155–157
ImageStation, 169
   photo books, creating, 174
importing images with photo album
    software, 119

incremental backups, 199
index number, printing by, 148
indoor photos
   lighting, working with, 183
   portraits, taking, 188
infinity focus mode, 54
InfoTrends Research Group, 132
infrared (IrDA) wireless devices,
   134
   mobile phone cameras with, 165
inkjet printers. *See also* printing
   borderless prints capabilities, 133
   colors, number of, 133
   Dell inkjet printers, 133
   direct printing from camera, 134
   duration of photos from, 198
   fading problem, 140
   operating systems, support for, 135
   resolution with, 132–133
   settings, choosing, 135–138
   speed for printing, 133
   steps for printing photos, 135–138
   storage media slots, 134
Instant Messaging (IM) photos, 154
interface options, 15. *See also* USB
    ports
   for inkjet printers, 133
   TV Out interface, 18
interlaced downloading, 155
interpolation, sensors using, 6
iPhoto 4, 122
   Kodak, printing pictures through, 169
   photo books, creating, 174
iris diaphragm, 44
iron-on transfer paper, 176
ISO equivalencies, 15–16
iTunes music with slideshows, 122

J

Jasc. *See also* Paint Shop Pro
   Paint Shop Photo Album, 123
jewel cases, 124
jewelry box with photo tiles,
   creating, 172

JPEG files
  artifacts in, 93
  EXIF data, storing, 196–198
  inexpensive cameras and, 18
  midrange cameras and, 10
  printers supporting, 146
  for Web page photos, 155

K

keychains with photos, creating, 172
keywords for images, assigning, 120
Kmart, printing at, 148
Kodak. *See also* **EasyShare cameras**
  docks from, 19
  Picture CD, importing images with, 119
  Picture Center Online, 169
Konica Minolta, 8

L

landscape mode, 54–55
  icon for, 54
landscape orientation, printing in, 138
lasso tool, 93
LCD indicators, 28
LCD screens, 23
  menu system, displaying, 24
  power conservation settings, 33
  waking up, 31
least expensive cameras, 8–9
lens caps, 22
  straps, 25
lens papers, 20, 23
lenses, 22
  as decision feature, 13
  dirt on, 23
  on least expensive cameras, 9
  on midrange cameras, 9
  on power on camera, 27
  for professional cameras, 11–12

light and lighting. *See also*
  aperture; backlighting; fill
  lighting; shutter speed; sunlight
  low-light pictures, 57–58
  for portraits, 187
  for subject, 183–184
lithium rechargeable batteries, 26
Long Time Exposure mode, 48
lossy format, 18
low-light pictures, 57–58
  icons for, 58
luggage tags with photos, creating, 172

M

Macintosh computers. *See also*
  iPhoto 4
  with digital media readers, 65
macro mode. *See* **close-up mode**
magnets with photos, creating, 172
Maxtor external drives, 199–200
megapixels, 11
megapixels (MP), 7
Memory Stick, 14
  inkjet printer slots for, 134
  ports for, 69
  printing directly from, 146
  USB storage card readers for, 64
menu system, displaying, 24
MF indicator, focus and, 42
Microsoft
  Digital Image Pro, 83
  Plus! Digital Media Edition, 20
Microsoft Scanner and Camera Wizard, 70
  transferring pictures with, 72–75
midrange cameras, 9–10
Minolta DiMAGE X20 Ultracompact Digital Camera, 8
MMC (MultiMediaCard), printing directly from, 146
mobile phone cameras
  printing directly from, 134
  working with, 162–164